Everyone Needs a Lyft

My Thirty-Day Odyssey as a Lyft Driver

Matthew V. Brown, Ph. D.

Library of Congress CataloginginPublication Data

Brown, Matthew, V.
Everyone needs a lyft : my thirty-day odyssey as a lyft driver /
Matthew V. Brown
p. cm.

ISBN 978-1-66785-935-4 (print)
ISBN 978-1-66785-936-1 (eBook)

1. Business 2. Management 3. Pandemic 4. Rideshare 5. Short Stories
I Title

Copyright Registration Number TXu 2-320-508

TABLE OF CONTENTS

Foreword by Esther Wojcicki

INTRODUCTION

EPILOGUE

This book is dedicated to the four women that continue to inspire me, Mia, Josie, Kaydonna, and Esther to be a better husband, father, son, and educator.

ACKNOWLEDGEMENTS

I am extremely grateful to those that helped me complete this first book. My wife, Mia first had the idea that during the pandemic quarantine, that I not retire but find ways to conduct research. My daughter, Josephine [Josie] suggested I try Lyft driving for something to do in the later period of the pandemic. My good friend, Esther Wojcicki recommended I combine the two: research the pandemic by collecting Lyft passenger stories shaping the collection into a book. Esther also convinced me to self-publish the book on Kindle Direct and avoid the painful challenges of landing a conventional publisher. My mother, Kaydonna Brown helped me painstakingly review and edit the story chapters reading every sentence and word learning that editing is every bit as laborious as writing.

I am indebted to my community of mentors and colleagues at the University of Michigan, Ann Arbor where I first became enamored with the study of organization--notably Marvin Peterson, Michael D. Cohen, Karl Weick, Jane Dutton, Susan Ashford, Amy Gillett, Patricia King, Sylvia Hurtado, Gretchen Spreitzer, Robert Quinn, Kim Cameron, John Branch, Maxim Sytch, Cheri Alexander, Melanie Barnett, Kent Youll, Caroline Tuet, Shahnaz Broucek, and Barb Kirby-Bloch. Thank you to Adam Grant and Daniel Pink for your suggestions and encouragement.

I appreciate the contributions of Paul Domish of Drifter Vans and Sean at Midas Auto Repair. My good friends, David Baker, Millie Chu, Kristen Gapske, Cynthia Scott, Dennis Jaffe, Ari Black, and special thanks to Cynthia Pepper.

At this point, I want to thank my two wonderful brothers, Mark and Marty Brown, who like me have wrestled and toiled through some serious life challenges with me, all while maintaining their sense of humor and brotherly affections. I want them to know that this book is theirs.

FOREWORD

It is 2022, and the world has changed in so many ways. One of them is ridesharing. LYFT and UBER have changed how we get from point A to point B in cities worldwide. I remember when ridesharing first started. I was invited to a party in Los Altos Hills, CA, to celebrate the naming. That was back in 2012, ten years ago. I remember thinking that LYFT was a clever name, and I still think so. I never understood UBER's meaning, so I had to look it up. Not many people know that it means My Unified Best Economical Ride. Ha ha. I prefer LYFT. In Silicon Valley, no one ever sees taxi drivers anymore; they all have become LYFT or UBER drivers.

As ridesharing was growing, I became more curious. I always wanted to know what it is like to be a rideshare driver and how passengers behave. What do they talk about? Or do they speak with the drivers during the ride? I know what it is like to be a passenger, but I don't know what it is like to pick up passenger after passenger all day long, to be a driver.

So, I had my chance when I met Matthew Brown, Ph. D., virtually while working for a small-ed tech company in Mountain View, CA. He was one of the faculty members who later decided to take on LYFT driving to supplement his faculty income. I was secretly happy about it since it was now my chance to find out what it was like. I encouraged him to write a book about it.

As a professor, Matthew knows how to interact with people, get their stories, organize information, and write. I could hardly wait to get him interested in writing about his experiences and the people he drove. As it turned out, it was easy to get him interested. He loved the idea of writing a book about Lyft passengers and gig work experiences, and what you are reading today is the wonderful result.

The people he describes represent a compelling cross-section of America. Each story stands on its own, yet there are common threads throughout the collection. The stories are presented in the order they occurred. It is a fascinating read about whom he picked up and how driving for Lyft changed him.

It is a significant challenge driving for five or more hours per day. It is hard on your body and your mind. Matthew explains in detail what happened to him and connects it to what happens to so many rideshare drivers worldwide. He shares thirty exciting and insightful stories about interacting with his passengers in this fantastic collection of short stories. It's a great read.

-Esther Wojcicki
July 2022

INTRODUCTION

"And what is the use of a book," thought Alice, "without pictures or conversations?"

- Lewis Carroll

The Covid-19 pandemic changed everything.

In the late summer of 2021, we were eighteen months into what felt like house arrest due to the spread of the Covid-19 virus. I was suitably concerned about contracting the virus, yet I enjoyed my time at home with my wife Mia after teaching as a professor for twenty years. That autumn, I started looking for something to do.

Lyft driving certainly wasn't the first type of work that came to mind. My wife, Mia, and our daughter, Josephine, ganging up on me during a late summer bonfire, started this entire adventure. Mia said, "Matt, you need to get out of the house and do something besides reading books and playing your guitar!" My daughter said, "Dad, you like to drive and talk to strangers. You enjoy hearing their stories and telling them yours." I agreed with them. "Why don't you look into Lyft driving?"

"Why in the world would I want to Lyft drive?" Well, three weeks later, here we are. For the past twenty years, I had been a professor of organizational behavior trained in applying social science theories to explain [and improve] workplace dynamics.

Then in the summer of 2020, I completed a three-year contract where my daughter attended college. The college was forced to cut back, and I became unemployed for what I thought would be one year. I collected unemployment insurance benefits for the first time. I had not worked to secure any future employment and had no immediate income-generating prospects.

It was surprisingly easy to become a Lyft driver. All I had to do was submit some identification documents and get my automobile inspected. That was the entire application process. No interviews, no exams, no training save watching a few videos about driving safety and how to avoid participating in sexual conversations, and no onboarding. After checking the boxes, I was good to Go Online and began accepting rides and delivering passengers to their requested destinations. My daughter called me that day and said I was officially a gig worker.

The events during my first week of Lyft driving transformed a casual diversion into a full-fledged research effort. Let me explain.

On the fifth day of Lyft driving, I received a phone call from my mentor, Esther Wojcicki. Surprise, the Godmother of Silicon Valley is one of my most cherished friends. What occurred on Day Five [October 1] is essential to the story. How I became Esther's friend and colleague is another story of serendipity itself. Suffice to say, Esther and I share many ideas about education, learning, student success, and how each phenomenon occurs.

She asked me what I was doing to pay my bills now that my social safety net [unemployment insurance] had ended a few weeks prior. She knew I might be struggling.

I was reluctant to tell Esther the truth because I didn't know how to explain how I went from a full-time business professor who taught management and organization to a lowly chauffeur or taxi driver. However, I caved and decided to come clean with her. I told her that I started Lyft driving a few days ago to make some money quickly and collect some good stories. I prepared myself for the sympathetic message, tough love, and clear rebuke that did not come. Instead, she said, "That's GREAT! Why don't you write about that? You are such a natural writer, Matthew." Are you collecting stories from passengers? I asked her if she had been speaking to my daughter?

Each chapter story contains a short commentary [400 words or less] except for chapter thirty. On one occasion, I shared a story with a passenger. I used pseudonyms to disguise ALL my storytelling participants except in one, Story Nineteen– A Close Call.

Wow, I sure didn't expect that response from you, Esther. She continued, "Now, I want an outline for a [book project] on Lyft passenger stories, gig work, and the social effects of the pandemic before you go to sleep tonight," demanded Esther, my new writer-mentor.

"Wait a minute! Am I the professor here? I give the assignments. Ha ha. Yet, of course, I defer to your better judgment." And we laughed. If you know Esther Wojcicki, you will understand why I did exactly what she told me to do [still do]. Esther knows what she is talking about when it comes to being successful.

I sent her an initial outline around 2:30 am, and she replied, "brilliant." Then I couldn't sleep. I woke my wife and told her that I felt like I had done something stupid. I think I just committed to writing a book for Esther.

"About what?" she said, half-awake. "Good luck with that." She turned over and went back to sleep. I was still awake at 7 am. I sipped a fourth cup of instant coffee, and suddenly the title of this book hit me like a rock in the forehead. The title is: Everyone Needs a Lyft: My Thirty-Day Odyssey as a Lyft Driver.

I quickly sent the title phrase to Esther for a response: A few hours later, I received a one-word message…perfect. This book would also be about strangers exchanging small gifts of empathy and goodwill. For each passenger that gave me a story [good or dull], I gave them more than a safe ride. I would share a small gift of helpful information, a networking opportunity, or the title of a learning resource.

The initial plan was that I would dutifully collect fifty or so stories from Lyft passengers during the first thirty days of driving. I would assemble from my notes an accurate interpretation of the conversational dialogues and evaluate them for quality and insight. I would focus on recording their pandemic experiences, work changes, personal disruptions, upheavals, innovations, and revelations. I was also looking for evidence of positive activity, such as adaptive ideas, actions, and examples of fortunate accidents (serendipity). I wanted to capture the experiences that inspired [lifted] people.

Everyone Needs a Lyft is a series of thirty passenger stories presented in chronological order. Some are verbatim conversations that occurred during their specific Lyft ride. Omitted were twenty stories that were considered redundant or not compelling enough stories. Many passengers betrayed what they endured during the pandemic. I aimed to ease passengers' distress and anger and lessen pain first and record a good story second. I focused on sharing goodwill and being a positive emissary for Lyft and my passengers' safety, health, and well-being.

Story One

Just Out of Prison

September 27, 2021

The famous inventor of lateral thinking, Edward De Bono, advised the Foreign Office in 2000 that he had a solution to the conflict in the Middle East. He argued that the entire sorry business might be partly due to people having low levels of zinc from eating unleavened bread. A known side-effect of having low zinc levels in one's blood was high levels of aggressive behavior. His answer was to ship hundreds of jars of Marmite (yeast extract) to arrest the zinc shortage in everyone's diet.

It was my first day of Lyft driving (third ride). I began this new adventure with no clear idea of what to expect or how to do it.

I accepted the third Lyft ride request for pickup at the Meijer grocery store in Ypsilanti, MI. Fortunately, the passenger pickup was just down the road from my second ride drop-off. Pulling into the parking lot, I slowly approached the store entrance. I pushed the Arrive button.

He had to be my next passenger, I thought. I quickly glanced at the name on the Lyft app: Derrick. He was a massive fellow, perhaps six/ eight or nine. He weighed about 300 lbs. Over-stuffed plastic bags dangled from each finger. How would he fit in my small car?

I guessed right. I could see how huge this man was getting out of the car to open the trunk lid. I tried to get a close look at him without arousing his suspicion.

Tattoos covered his entire body. Tattoos surrounded his forehead, his neck, his arms, and legs. He even had tattoos on both ears, reminding me of the character in Ray Bradbury's 1951 book, the Illustrated Man.

Wearing gray synthetic gym shorts below his knees and cheap rubber flip-flops on his feet, he amusingly looked like he was headlining a WWF-Sumo wrestling match. However, unlike a sumo wrestler, he didn't have a tight hair bun with a giant wooden hairpin holding it together. He was completely bald.

I jumped out of the car to open the car boot. Derrick slowly walked around the vehicle and released each bag, ensuring he did not disturb the contents. His cargo was an assortment of snack foods. He had pop tarts, Life cereal, assorted crackers, jars of jams and jellies, pickled herring, dried fruits, and other breakfast-type foods. There must have been four or five kinds of Little Debbie cakes in two bulging packages. To me, it certainly was a lot of junk food!

After arresting his fingers from the plastic bag holds, he stood up. It was then that I realized how big this man was. I am six-four and weigh about 235 lbs. and no small person. Yet I still felt a bit nervous standing beside him. What a fascinating human being he turned out to be with a powerful tale to tell. Here is his story.

Derrick's first words spoken directly to me were:

P: Most people when they first meet me are afraid of me. He said this while staring at me. He closed the trunk lid.

M: Well, I am a pretty big guy. I grew up on the east side of Detroit. I am not afraid of anyone, I said rather proudly. He looked up into the cloudy grey sky as if he heard someone else speaking.

P: Good, I am glad we got that out of the way.

M: Where are we headed? He held up his hand. He showed me two words written inside his palm, McNichols and Telegraph.

P: Detroit, do you know where these two streets meet?

M: Sure, I grew up about five miles from there. It is about thirty minutes from here on the NW side of Detroit.

As Derrick got into the back seat, I pushed the front passenger seat forward. He had difficulty bending himself into my VW Jetta. I apologized for having such a small car. Once he got settled, we proceeded to the I-94 expressway heading east. Derrick stared at me in the rear-view mirror.

P: Listen, I have something important to tell you.

M: What's that?

P: I was released from prison two hours ago.

M: Two hours ago, huh? That explains the groceries. Congratulations, you're a free man!

P: Have you ever read Dante's Inferno?

M: Yes, we studied it in one of my undergraduate literature courses. I know the story quite well. It's a poem about traveling through hell.

P: When I went into prison, we were in the first circle of hell. When the Covid came, we dropped down to the eighth circle. For the next thirty minutes, I will tell you precisely what the eighth circle of hell is about.

I thought to myself: OMG, is this what Lyft driving is like, passengers telling me stories about hell?

P: Six months ago today, I received my release date. The next day I got sick with the Covid. It started with a terrible headache. Then I started throwing up. I hadn't thrown up since I was a kid. Then I got a fever. They put me in a cold bath in the prison infirmary. By midnight, I was on a ventilator fighting for my life. I thought I was going to die in that damn prison.

Derrick told me the Covid-19 virus hit the entire prison first in November of 2020. However, things got worse in the spring of 2021. Everyone seemed to fall ill that spring. A few dozen men died in the infirmary during that first week. The early dead were older inmates incarcerated for most of their adult lives. The next wave seemed to take the healthy too. The guards kept that information from the inmate population early on. The rumors were worse than the truth, but the truth always comes out.

P: I was lucky to be alive. The lockdown happened on April 22. We lost our one-hour yard time. Then the kitchen closed down. It was solitary confinement. We were on limited water and delivered lousy food rations to our cells daily. It was horrible because the food was worse than it usually was. I was one of the first to land in the infirmary. It was cold and not very clean. Back in the block, one man could shower at a time with two guards watching over him. Get the covid, no shower. Take three minutes to wipe yourself with a damp washcloth and then back to your cell.

P: The guards started getting scared. Everyone grew angrier and acted meaner. It was a terrible formula. There were hourly fights with guards, two of my cell brothers got injured, then got the Covid virus, and one died in the next two days. I was on a ventilator for a week, but I made it through. They took me off it and sent me right back to my cell.

P: Imprisoned men get used to how things work quickly or suffer abuse. It is day after day of the same routines. Covid-19 changed all of our routines. That made being there even more unbearable. My worst day was when they closed the prison kitchen. I worked in the bakery. It took five years to get that job. All of a sudden, it was gone.

P: Many of us did not eat for days. Men went crazy from not sleeping. Others cursed their last profane death rap. All kinds of gruesome noises filled the prison air. Groaning with pain, some men cried out and screamed for hours. It wasn't music. It was pure suffering.

P: Men did disgusting and horrible things to get out of their cells. One man broke his arm between the cell bars to get to the infirmary, while another threw his feces at the guards. The place went insane. I'm never going back. I'll die first.

P: The toughest thing was watching my cellmates die. Some I didn't care about, but a few I did. How pitiful the place quickly became. No one knows what goes on in prison. No one cares. He admitted he was scared to death at times. We pulled into the parking lot of a rundown motel on Detroit's northwest side. Half of the rooms were missing doors and littered with trash.

M: Are you sure this is where you want to be? It is not a very good neighborhood. I can take you anywhere in Detroit on me.

P: It was the only place available to stay within a half-mile of where I grew up. I will make it work.

We got out of the car and walked around toward the trunk. Derrick reached out his enormous hand and grabbed mine. It was like shaking hands with a person wearing a baseball glove. His fingers were like sausages.

M: My God, where did you get those hands? You have hands like a blacksmith.

P: I don't usually tell people this, but you seem like a straight-up guy. Like I told you, I worked in the prison kitchen as a baker. My grandmother taught me how to bake when I was fourteen.

M: Wow, what do you like to bake?

P: Bread is my specialty. I can bake 36 different kinds of Bread.

M: Wow, I didn't even know there were 36 different kinds of Bread. That is quite a talent.

P: I want to thank you for not asking me what I did to get into prison.

M: You're welcome. It didn't seem like an appropriate question to ask you.

P: Well, I was raised by stupid people. They taught me a lot of stupid things. So, I became stupid as a result, angry and stupid. Then I did something horrible and wound up in prison. I'm not going to tell you exactly what I did. That was in 2006. I'm never going back. I'll die first.

M: Good, don't go back.

P: I will die first.

M: 2006, huh? That is 15 years. That is a long time to be locked up. But you are what, 38 or 39 years old? You still have much life ahead of you. Please make the most of it. Why don't you start a bakery? I bet people would travel hundreds of miles to meet you. I am nobody. You are the great Baker that will make your grandmother proud, Derrick. You know she looks down at you, wondering what you will do with the rest of your life.

P: Yeah, that might work, but I lost my sense of smell and my sense of of taste after getting the Covid. And besides, I don't feel that free at all.

M: You will get that all back. I wish I could help you more, Derrick. Hey, have you ever heard of Ray Bradbury, the author? He wrote a book in 1951 called the Illustrated Man. I think you might enjoy reading it. Imagine the story of a man with tattoos all over his body just like you. He travels the world telling people the history and future of humanity. Maybe this story will inspire you. It inspired me when I read it.

P: Hmmm. What was his name again?

M: Ray Bradbury. Here is a pen. Let's write his name on your other palm. Put the book title in your cell phone contacts too. Look up his name when you can. Here, Can I help you with your groceries?

P: No, but thanks for the ride and the conversation. You are a good man.

He almost smiled as he gathered up his bags of groceries. But he didn't and lumbered off toward the motel.

****

It would have been easy to reject Derrick's request for a Lyft ride based only on his menacing appearance. Yet, I am just not like that. Imagine how difficult it was for him to be released from prison at any time, especially during the Covid-19 pandemic. I dropped Derrick off at a dreadful place on Detroit's west side.

It is important to note that the idea of writing a book about Lyft driving or even seriously gathering passenger stories had not yet taken shape in my mind. He was my third passenger on my first day of Lyft driving.

His horrific story rattled me as I pulled away from the motel parking lot. I had to get the story down verbatim before I forgot it, so I rushed home. It was the kind of story one hears once in a lifetime. Whoever thinks about what goes on in prison? I assumed terrible things occurred there. I thought his story needed to be shared. I wanted to tell it.

When Derrick mentioned Dante, I was impressed by his referencing the famous poem about hell. How little I knew about being confined in a place likened to torture. T. S. Eliot wrote that it is better not to know anything about Dante's Inferno before reading it.

For some strange reason, I also thought of Homer's Odyssey during this ride. Odysseus worked with his post-war release leading to his return home. He became restless and longed for a new adventure. Odysseus soon sets off to talk to strangers and gather new stories. He meets a Cyclops and uses his wit and cunning to escape from the monster. I had no such experience with Derrick.

We have all experienced some small measure of what Derrick went through during the pandemic. I suddenly wanted to know how people adapted to quarantining and working at home. Lyft rides became my new classroom.

When I called my daughter later that first day, she suggested that I collect passenger stories because she wanted me to enjoy doing this work.

I drove more than five hours that first day and earned $38.00. At least I collected a few good stories if I didn't make enough money driving. Like Derrick, it was good enough to simply end our periods of confinement, his extreme and mine a minor inconvenience.

Story Two

True Grit

September 28, 2021

There is a Yiddish word I cannot pronounce, "tzebrokhnkayt," which means "the quality of broken-heartedness that gives strength in healing." Its essence means that "we carry our shattered pieces with us." The essential bit is that tzebrokhnkayt is not something that needs quick fixing; it is instead honored. It means that we are obligated to gather up, tend to and keep the pain while taking up the work of healing.

"Just after the explosion, I saw my mother's face. It was not God or Jesus reaching out to save me. It was her love that saved me in the final moment."

- David

On my second Lyft driving day, I picked up a US Army veteran at the VA Hospital. I watched him as he was wheelchair riding up to my car. To my surprise, he then stood up. He looked at me smiling while struggling to take a step forward. I wanted to help him, but I stopped myself. It was clear he wanted to navigate getting into my car himself. So, he did.

M: Hello there, David! Where are we headed today?

P: I am visiting my sister's house for a few days. It is a kind of experiment. My doctors want to see how I handle going out on my own. Dr. Schelling wants to know if I have any grit left in me. Ha Ha.

M: Well, you look like you have plenty of grit left.

P: Yeah, maybe I am just gritty to the bone? I have had seven surgeries in the last four years. An IED exploded under my armored vehicle.

It messed me up all right nearly lost this leg. My left hand was too badly damaged to save. Now I have a robotic hand.

M: Like the Six Million Dollar man on 1970s TV! Sorry, I am betraying my age.

P: Well, maybe not six million. Still alive and kicking. Hey, I have heard of that TV show. It is still on cable TV, I think.

M: We are lucky to have you back, David. Thanks for your service.

P: You're welcome. My mom is the one with grit. She was the one that kept me going through all this. I was trained well as a soldier, but she taught me how to fight.

P: I watched her fight her last battle behind a Goddamn glass wall. She was so brave. She looked at me with such overwhelming love and grace. I kept trying to rise out of my wheelchair. I wanted to hug her the way she hugged me when I returned from Iraq. One of the last things she told me was to keep fighting, God is right beside you, and I will be beside God. I never bought into much of the God stuff. I sure believed in her. And when she passed, I needed help.

P: I still had a bunch of battles fighting to relearn all the daily things we take for granted. It was so hard learning how to eat again, putting the food in my mouth, and holding a damn fork. I wanted to quit because it never seemed to get any better, week after week, month after month. I found some help from the people of her church. They showed me their grit.

P: I am so much better now at those simple things. Grit helps me stay with the simple things. Three years ago, I got back from the hospital in Germany. My mom picked up from where the doctors and therapists left off. They had to keep me moving all the time. My mom made a simple game of it. She is the one with grit. She never quits, and she would not let me leave. I couldn't let her down. She made me want to play.

M: I am sorry for your loss. You could be a "grit consultant" teaching people how to keep from quitting. A lot of people could use that very instruction, especially today.

P: Is there even such a job? Never heard of such work, but you are right. I bet I would be pretty good at it. I wonder what I teach and to whom?

M: It would be great if you could talk to high school students. Talk to them about how you muster the courage and perseverance to keep going after experiencing your most challenging tests. Teach them what to do when everything is telling them to quit.

M: I can imagine some of the lessons you learned in the Army. What do these lessons teach you now that your tour as a soldier is complete? You were severely wounded. How do you approach the challenges of life directly? I think your answers are valuable knowledge. Not everyone will face what you face every day, but I bet they will find true inspiration in your story. You have a great gift to share with younger folks.

P: You think so, huh?

M: Think of grit as being your new curriculum. Your story has important lessons to share about determination and resilience. Have you ever read Tuesdays with Morrie by Mitch Albom? It is one of my favorites. Filled with so many gems, Morrie tells Mitch that "giving makes him feel alive while taking feels like dying." People don't often think about how giving is vital to keep living. We know that those with grit are determined to live. That is where you begin.

P: Did I tell you I needed to learn how to be physically active all over again after my injuries put me on my back for several months. Yet that was not the most challenging time. That time came later after I had made substantial progress. I started to feel better and didn't know what to do. I got comfortable being disabled. I had sunk into self-pity and self-blame and got depressed. My mother encouraged me to write about that, and it helped. And another thing, I am not sure today's young people realize how much they sit. Now I sit a lot less. I do sit in a wheelchair to move around some, but I also play basketball in it three times a week. I learned that physical exercise had much to do with my mental well-being.

I changed my eating habits in dramatic ways. I eat a lot healthier now than I did when I was in the Army. I ate too much fast food before my injuries; most of it was worse for me than Army food.

M: Ha Ha. That's funny.

P: More exercise and a better diet equal a healthier lifestyle. We push each other forward. We don't talk about injuries or disabilities. It is like military training only without the Drill Sargent leading! In many important ways, I feel better.

M: Now, that is what young people need to hear. They need to learn the benefits of what is healthy and positive from someone exactly like you.

M: I bet you could help younger people learn how to thrive during the pandemic. Developing grit is a learning process. It could toughen them up for future challenges. It might even save their lives.

M: We are coming to the end of our ride, but I want to give you a small gift for riding with me, David. I want to tell you about some research on this subject you might find interesting by Angela Duckworth. She studies how grit develops in people and how we can increase it in our characters. She would want to hear your story. If you have a minute, let me get you her contact information. Oh, and I am probably not supposed to do this, but here is my email address.

I want to ask you a few more questions if you have the time. I am curious about how people develop grit. You are the living evidence!

****

Derrick and David were very different. Yet life had presented both with similar challenges that made my circumstance seem like a holiday. It was anyone's guess who had developed more grit.

David moved our conversation beyond how he suffered by immediately sharing with me challenges without inviting me to help. Instead, he shared what got him through demanding times. What got me through my demanding times? I didn't know, so I listened carefully.

In the follow-up conversation with David, he revealed something that many of us will never know as he does. He told me that the worst experience in combat was watching fellow soldiers die in battle. It was maddening and broke David apart.

Every time one of his brothers was killed, he vowed to avenge them. He would swear before his enemies and shout out take me, you F _ _ _ _ _ cowards. Then a fellow soldier showed him another way to deal with the loss. This other way had to do with grit.

Before his "accident," with help, he developed the kind of grit born of courage and resolve. I envied him in a way. He was full of courage. The courage came from from learning how to keep friends from harm. A second form of courage came from knowing how to stay alive so that he could keep friends from harm. He told me that he found some success in that. And yet, his highest level of courage came from struggling with rehabiitation knowing it would last the rest of his life. He told me he drew strength from his mother's love and built tenacity that kept him from losing hope. David described how his mother held everything together. I could not help but think about families enduring the pandemic. Who was holding them together? I wondered how thousands and thousands of families were keeping things together while losing loved ones to the Covid-19 virus.

Like the soldiers, ordinary people watch helplessly as loved ones succumb to the Covid-19 virus. The survivors develop grit. I asked David if he thought how grit might help me get through the pandemic. He said that if he knew more about my challenges, he could encourage my development. Good answer.

I told David about Angela Duckworth's research identifying five core components of grit: courage, conscientiousness, perseverance, resilience, and passion. He later wrote me an email saying that he was busy working on a podcast for other wounded veterans and their families focusing on how to develop grit.

Story Three

Parental Control

September 29, 2021

"Psychologists call it 'learned helplessness' when a person believes, as I did during my youth, that the choices I made years ago would not affect the outcomes in my life."

- J. D. Vance, Hillbilly Elegy

The setting of this story is Parent's Weekend in Ann Arbor. Parents visit their children attending college to check their overall conditions and have fun. The Universities take these weekends seriously as scheduled events help improve alum-university bonds and garner future donations. Two middle-aged university alums have traveled to visit their children and perhaps something more. Close friends in college, then business partners, and now their children virtually attend the same university simultaneously.

M: Hi Carol [C], welcome to my Ann Arbor-Ypsilanti Lyft Riding adventure! [D] is passenger Doug

C: Hello, Matthew. Good to meet you. We have a two-stop ride, OK?

M: Sure, no worries.

C: I am here visiting on Parent's Weekend. My daughter goes to UM.

M: That is wonderful. Where to today?

Carol rifled through her purse and withdrew some lipstick.

C: I'm sorry, what? I am so nervous. I am picking up an old UM friend at the Marriot and meeting my business partners. Our investor group is visiting a Recreational Vehicle [RV] center nearby.

M: No need to explain.

C: Everyone I know sends their kids to UM. It is a tradition and has been for several generations. I was here twenty years ago. The University of Michigan works for us. We are all here with our old college friends. It is like a big reunion party! Maybe I can keep my daughter from staying out all night drinking? Parents are primarily from northern California, Chicago, and Long Island, NY.

M: You may be right. I happen to be an ex-faculty member at UM Ross School of Business in Management and Organization.

C: One of my business partners earned her MBA here and now owns a toy store. She was expanding because everyone was buying games and puzzles, etc. She saw her business nearly double in six months! Another partner owned a small chain of bookstores that were struggling in 2020. Now, she is seeing double-digit growth and is hiring new people. Everyone must find new things to do at home.

M: The pandemic hit everyone differently. I have friends who own restaurants that had to close their doors or scale down their operations because they had to close their dining rooms. Without carryout and delivery services, they would all be going bankrupt.

C: Well, I should not say this, but we are doing great. My husband's family owns a medical supply company. Now they manufacture masks, but you don't want to offend the neighbors too much. People are desperate. They get angry when you start talking about making a lot of money during the pandemic. We live in a suburban part of Chicago. You can tell who is doing well and who isn't. The first sign is the landscaping. The prosperous have their sculped yards and new Cadillac Escalades or Porsche Cayans. The struggling folks are riding to work on Lyft, Ha Ha.

M: That's funny.

C: We only talk with the winners because they only share the good news. That is why I come to events like Parent's Weekend. I get to see who is winning and losing.

M: OK, I appreciate your honesty. Here is the Marriot.

C: Here is my first stop. I run into more of my neighbors here in UM-Ann Arbor than when I am home. Oops, there is Doug.

M: Hello Doug, nice to meet you.

Doug and Carol hugged intensely. You could tell they were fond of each other. I felt embarrassed watching them. Doug sure had this calming effect on Carol. I tried not to stare at them.

M: OK, on to the [other] Marriot at the Ypsilanti Eagle Crest Resort. A great place. It is one of the jewels of Ypsilanti, MI.

D: Thanks, Driver Matt.

Ugghh. I realized I no longer existed. I was this robot named Driver Matt. After a couple of awkward minutes, I decided to ask them a question.

M: How long have you two been married?

They both stopped and looked up and began laughing.

D: Oh, us, we're not married. I mean not to each other. Carol and I are close friends. We met here at UM years ago. We belong to the same investment group. Carol's husband's family does some business with my company.

M: Carol was sharing some things before we picked you up. I

apologize. It is none of my business. I am an ex-faculty member at UM, where I taught organizational behavior. I retired and started Lyft driving a few days ago to collect passenger stories and write about the experience.

D: Wow, that sounds interesting. I guess she told you both our eldest daughters are attending UM. Parent's Weekend. However, this year is a bit different. Our investment group is all here to decide on a significant deal acquisition. We all got tired of the virtual meetings.

M: Yes, Carol mentioned that you are looking at a Recreational Vehicle Center to purchase.

D: Yes, that is correct.

The two refocused their attention on their phones. I assumed the conversation had ended. I could tell they wanted to resume their sharing. I left them alone. I wasn't sure I had a compelling passenger story here. Then something interesting happened a phone call.

D: Hello, Julia [my daughter]? What's up?

[Julia on the phone]: "Dad, what time is your investor meeting? Do Jocelyn and I have time to go to Bubble Tea?"

Doug: You mean the meeting or the dinner? The meeting is at 3 pm, and the dinner is at six. Doug then put his index finger to his mouth and said, Shhhh.

[Julia on phone]: "Where are you now?"

D: Back to the hotel to change clothes. I will meet you in front of the bank downtown in an hour and a half."

[Julia on phone]: "That's cutting it pretty close. Everyone else will already be there."

D: I will schedule a Lyft ride. Don't worry, and I will be there."

D: Good-Bye.

We pulled into the Eagle Crest Resort as Doug said goodbye to his daughter. He looked at Carol and smiled. They both got out of the car. Doug motioned to Carol and circled the vehicle approaching my window. I opened it to hear him.

D: You are Lyft driving to collect passenger stories? You don't use people's real names, do you?

M: No, sir. I use pseudonyms. I don't think there is a compelling story here.

D: Thanks. Here take this.

M: I would rather not.

D: Go on, take it. Go Blue. For being a good sport.

M: Keep it. Goodbye Doug. Best of luck with the acquisition.

Parent's Weekend in early autumn is an opportunity for parents with the means to live vicariously through their college-age children— the word vicarious means to experience something through another person. In ecclesiastical terms, vicar means a substitute for a parson or priest. I am not my Lyft passengers' priest or their moral conscience, but I did have to resist moralizing during this ride.

Most of my Lyft passengers were humble and gracious. These passengers were flippant about privilege and wealth. Carol revealed so much about her personal life, and I was surprised when she suggested the pandemic had brought her family good fortune. Their family businesses doubled in size while others around them closed their doors. The pandemic reshuffled the commerce card deck, and they had drawn one of the winning hands.

These Parent Weekend passengers were amusing at first. Finally, they offended me. What do they call when someone tries to buy your complicity? I didn't care about their peccadillos.

Doug told me how much his older children charged to his credit cards during their first year at the University, while Carol boasted about the new car she bought for her daughter. They paid for spring break cruises and lavish trips abroad. The pandemic didn't seem to affect them adversely.

When Doug stepped over to chat with me, I tried to convey indifference as he held out a twenty-dollar bill. As I looked at the money, I felt incensed. I almost said she's waiting for you, Doug. I didn't. I didn't take the money either. I drove off.

I dropped Carol and Doug off at the resort. I felt like screaming out loud. I didn't want to have anything more to do with these passengers. They acted smug with me, and I was offended. It was challenging to suspend judgment entirely when I engaged with passengers that offended my core sensibilities or ethics. Then I reminded myself, who am I to judge?

We all have flaws. I was struck by how these people betrayed their genuine selves to a stranger. However, I am no vicar. Carol was simply proud of her family, and Doug felt guilty about his. I felt guilty, too, for judging them so harshly. Perhaps we all needed to go to confession?

Story Four

Dr. Jekyll Meets Mr. Hyde

September 30, 2021

"With every day, and from both sides of my intelligence, the moral and the intellectual, I thus drew steadily nearer to the truth, by whose partial discovery I have been doomed to such a dreadful shipwreck: that man is not truly one, but truly two."

- Robert Louis Stevenson

One passenger became my first duplicate ride, and the two rides with the same passenger occurred on the same day. He is an older man lost in a lonely cycle of drunkenness and self-imposed misery. He doesn't know how to do anything else. He describes an endless search for an old friend in years past who was the one who could listen. The more he searches, the drunker he gets. The drunker he gets, the less likely he will find this imaginary friend.

Part 1: First Ride with Sean

M: Hello Sean, Where to?

P: Headed to my favorite pub to meet my mate for a late breakfast!

M: Sounds good. What is your mate's name?

P: Ahhh, the old goat. His name is Conor. A good Irishman and a splendid sham [friend] he is. We have known each other for half a century, mind you. Your given name is aye, Matthew? An old Hebrew name, a biblical name!

M: Yes, sir. It means gifted. It is with rare talents and worldly wisdom that I am blessed.

I pulled into the parking lot. A small group of men stood there arguing. I thought about canceling the ride, and then I spotted Sean from earlier that morning.

P: Better than early gifts from the Devil.

M: Where is this pub? Over on Huron Street. I must get there before noon to get a good seat for what they call brunch. They make a pretty good pub brunch. It is the only meal I can eat today.

Sean was an Old-World Irishman. Yet, I didn't want to think he was the stereotype Irish pub crawler with a drinking problem. I asked him what he did in his career.

P: Well, I worked for the automobile industry until I injured my foot. A lift truck ran over one of my feet and crushed four toes. It pretty much ended my working career. You notice I walk with a cane. It is pure luck that I can walk at all. I had a good run. I worked for a company called Budd Wheel in Detroit for twenty-five years.

M: Hey, that's amazing. My grandfather worked at Budd Wheel back in the 1950s. He was a welder. He got lung cancer and died when I was seven. He always told me that he would teach me to weld, but I was not interested in learning that art.

P: Yes, I am like your old granddad because I can weld anything too. Well, except my family matters. Hmmm. Hmmm. Here it is. Right when it opens. I hope you meet up with your friend for a pleasant visit. OK, Matthew, as they say in the old country, "Remember, two people shorten the road!"

M: My grandfather used to say that. Good luck to you, Sean.

****

Part 2. Second Ride with Sean (on the same day): Dr. Jekyll Meets Mr. Hyde.

Again, I hit the last ride button as it was 9 pm. The ride request was from another bar, and this time it was across town away from my home.I pulled into the parking lot. A small group of men stood there arguing. I thought about canceling the ride, and then I spotted Sean from earlier that morning.Sean's face was bloody, and his shirt was ripped open. I looked at the name on the Lyft app. It said, Bill. As they all turned around, I yelled out that I was a Lyft driver looking for Bill [B].

B: I'm Bill. Could you please get this old fool out of here? I ordered the Lyft ride for him.

M: Who gets the ride?

B: The little guy there. His name is Sean. He must leave before I call the cops.

P: Hey, who are you calling a little guy, you big f*#king pile of horseshit. He's the one who is shitfaced and calling everyone names.

B: Get him out of here.

M: I know this guy. Come on Sean, let's go home.

I am a big guy, 6' 4" tall and 230 lbs. I usually don't bother serving intoxicated people, and if they seem out of order from drinking or smoking, I cancel them before they get in my car. So, most people don't mess with me. Something told me that I should break my rule and give Sean a ride home. He didn't even recognize me.

I told Bill that I knew Sean and would help get him out. So, I got out of my car and walked up to Sean. As I approached him, he drew up his fists. I tried not to laugh because he was serious.

M: Hey Sean, it is time to shorten the road.

He looked at me cockeyed and blinked a few times.

P: Do I know you?

M: Yeah, I gave you a ride just this morning.

P: Bullshit, Conor brought me here.

M: OK, Conor brought you. Now, I must give you a ride home.

P: I must meet Conor at Powell's Pub.

M: We're at Powell's. He's not here.

P: Damn you! Conor will kick your ass. He must be at the Ale House.

M: OK, let's find him.

Sean got in the car and muttered that Powell's was a hell hole, and they didn't treat him well. I wondered how many times this drama occurred over the last few weeks, months. Perhaps every other day? I simply wanted to help Sean and try and get him to call it a night and go home. I asked him if he had Conor's phone number? He said he would call him.

Again, I looked at the GPS. The destination was a nearby residential address. I recognized the apartment complex. So, I decided to drive there quietly. When the phone answered, a woman spoke.

[Woman on the phone]: Hello? Sean? Is that you again?

P: Where is Conor? Put him on the phone, damn you.

[Woman on the phone]: Where are you? Conor is long gone. He is never coming back. You've been drinking. Stop calling me. Click.

P: Bitch.

We stopped at Sean's address, and he grumbled incoherently. He didn't put up much of a fight. I asked him if I could do anything for him.

P: No. I must go and find Conor.

M: I know. I know.

****

After this ride, I wanted to go home and spend time with my wife. I wouldn't say I like to drive after 9 pm, not because I expect there to be more intoxicated passengers requesting Lyft rides or that I will have to endure poor behavior or possible danger. I don't see that well in the dark. Driving at night is an unpleasant challenge. I remained puzzled after dropping Sean off. Sure, he was intoxicated and all, but relatively harmless. I could not figure out why meeting Conor was so important to Sean. I decided to inquire further.

I drove one block, then I called Bill back at the pub. I told him I was the Lyft driver that picked up Sean. I didn't have to call him, but I was curious about Conor and Sean's relationship. Maybe it was none of my business. I also wanted to see if there was a good story in all this. Bill told me that Conor was Sean's friend from his old automotive days. They accidentally ran into each other and started coming into the pub every couple weeks. Sean loved this guy, and they always had a good time "shooting the shit" about the old days. You know how these old guys get sentimental. The pub is a safe place to do that.

I think Conor got the covid-19 virus last year and died suddenly. Sean didn't find out for a few weeks that he had lost his only true friend. I told Bill that I was sorry to hear that. "You can't replace old friends," he said. I ended the phone call and just sat there in my car. I thought about the old friends I had lost in recent years.

Naïve people may think rideshare is primarily about providing safe passage for the inebriated and non-driving hooligans each night as they drink silly. I think of it as returning people home who sometimes get lost or overdo drinking, or smart people who avoid the dangers and dire consequences possible while driving unsober or high, given that recreational marijuana is now legal.

The Irish are fond of saying, "When we drink, we get drunk. When we get drunk, we fall asleep. When we fall asleep, we commit no sins. When we commit no sins, we go to Heaven."

Story Five

Urgent Care

October 1, 2021

"There are two ways of spreading light. You can be the candle, or you can be the mirror that reflects what shines."

- Edith Wharton

Several hospital personnel watched us from behind the glass walls. One of the nurses brought an older woman in a wheelchair to my car. As I helped the woman passenger into the car, she looked at me, forcing a faint smile. She looked exhausted, and her face was full of anguish and tears. She mumbled something that I could not quite hear. It sounded like she said, "Mera Pyar is gone."

M: Who is gone? I asked.

P: My love," she murmured.

M: I am so sorry to hear that.

P: I am alone now.

This poor woman lost her husband of 57 years to the Covid-19 virus the day before. She looked so frail. I immediately got out of the car to help her when I pulled up. She ever so slowly approached the vehicle, pushing her walker forward.

M: Don't you have any family here to help you? I asked.

P: No, Oh no. We have only been here in America for only two years. We are from Hyderabad, India. We came here so my husband could get his kidney treatments.

P: He got the Covid-19 virus. We both had it. My husband got sick almost immediately. I didn't. Now, I am exhausted. Maybe we could stop? Could I get some food?

M: Sure, what kind of food would you like to get?

P: There is an Indian restaurant called Cardamon on the north side of Ann Arbor. They have the food I like, and she started crying again.

M: I think it is on the way. I must stop the Lyft app tracking for this ride.

P: You don't have to do that, she said.

M: Yes, I do, I insisted. Lyft won't care. They make enough money off me.

P: Don't you like Lyft driving? My husband wanted to try it. He loved to drive, and I talked him out of it.

M: Yes, I like it for a bit of a break, but I am still a business professor. Driving might be dull and repetitive if I weren't collecting passenger stories for a book. Don't get me wrong. This ride is not boring.

M: Having passengers like you that I can help makes this worthwhile. Is this the restaurant?

P: Yes, I think so. Here is my card. Can you go in and get me some food?

I went in and summoned the manager. I told him that I was a Lyft driver that picked up an older woman that lost her husband to Covid-19 yesterday. He said he was sorry. I told him I wanted to order some food for her to take home and that I would pay for it. I put in my order. Then he said, look, I can give you half off for the two meals. Here is another coupon for her to come and have another meal on us when she is up to it.

M: This is very generous of you. I am writing a book about Lyft driving. I will tell other Lyft passengers about your generosity.

I gathered up the food and went back to my car. The woman was sleeping soundly, and I didn't want to wake her up, but because I turned off the Lyft app, I had no GPS to guide me to her destination. So, I woke her, and she was startled.

M: Here is your food and your credit card, I said. He didn't charge me for the food. Where are we going now?

P: The senior home on Bluff Street north of downtown Ann Arbor.

It started raining, and it was already dark. I was getting tired, having driven for about five hours. It took 30 minutes to find the senior center because it was on a hill surrounded by huge bushes and trees and not visible from the street. On the third pass, the woman went there. There it is. I pulled up to the front door, and the place looked empty. I helped with her walker. We proceeded to the door that opened automatically. She sat down in the lobby. A woman appeared from inside the senior home. [W]

W: Can I help you?

M: Yes, hi, my name is Matthew, and I am her Lyft driver. My passenger told me this is where she lives.

W: I don't recognize her. What is her name?

M: I was a little confused. The woman didn't live there. She lived at another senior home, and this is where her friend lived that she visited last month. I am sorry, but the woman inside says you don't live here.

P: I want to see my friend and then go home.

I went back in and explained the situation. The woman in the senior home was very gracious. She said she would try and find her friend and summon her to come down to the lobby. I watched the two women talk and hug, cry and cry for nearly 30 minutes. The senior home reception person went outside and had a smoke. I didn't know what to do except wait for the visit to end. I felt so miserable.

****

The fifth day of Lyft driving was like the previous four, except I started late. When I pulled up to the hospital entrance for what I thought would be my last ride of the day, the valet supervisor told me to park out of the way and wait. I felt nervous waiting because I didn't know how rideshare worked at the hospital. No one told me that patients get released; a social worker requests a Lyft ride, so their health insurance covers the cost. I waited ten extra minutes. Then I decided to circle the complex so others could have my spot.

My passenger was an elderly woman distraught. She moved toward my car, whimpering and muttering. My heart sank. I felt sick. Where was this woman's family, I thought? As I was helping this frail woman, barely able to lift her head, a nurse appeared and gave me a note with the address where I was to drive her. I turned to her and accepted the letter offering a puzzled look, and she mirrored the same look back. I realized that they were passing her on to me. It was like they were saying, "OK, Matt, you take her from here."

Imagine you just lost the most critical person in the world to a viral disease, and no one knows where it came from or how it works. All you know is that it took your lifelong love and partner. Broken with grief and despair, you must face the world alone.

One thing was clear. I was heading into unknown Lyft Driver territory with this ride. I did the best I could to help her. I got her food, and I tried to console her knowing it was like putting a bandage on a mortal wound. Lost in her grief, I wanted to get her home as quickly as possible. I wanted her to know the kindness of strangers.

At the beginning of the ride, I didn't even know what made my passenger so upset until she told me. I was determined to give her some little relief as I struggled to end a difficult day of driving. There were times I felt helpless during the pandemic period. This experience filled me with emotion and ended with some resolve. My fifth day of driving ended, and I resolved to practice empathy during future Lyft rides.

Story Six

Drive-Thru Open

October 2, 2021

The fast-food drive-thru may have originated at a chain of restaurants called the Pig Stand in Texas in 1921. However, according to a competing story, the first American drive-thru lane opened at a bank in St. Louis, MO September 22, 1930. Rumor had it that the first time anyone yelled, Get a move on, will you please? from a motorized vehicle occurred at that same bank later that day.

-History.com

    I woke up Saturday with a new sense of purpose. Esther suggested that I transform what I was initially doing [Lyft driving] into a research project. I would collect great passenger stories and write a book! So, I began with a set schedule - driving for five hours and writing for two.

    This passenger story takes us into the middle of the drive-thru deluge. It informed me who lost and who won in the local restaurant business. It helps to explain how food delivery services grew swiftly from delivering food to those in quarantine [at home] or in their cars during the second year of the Covid-19 pandemic.

    Ann Arbor [A2] is Michigan's village of trees. I came here because of the University, but I stayed because of its natural beauty and the healthy lifestyle. Autumn colors were nearing their peak. I drove around A2 that sultry October morning and hesitated to go online and resume Lyft driving. I headed toward the north side of the UM Campus. I noticed the extremely long lines at the fast-food drive-thrus. A few of the lines even extended into the adjacent street. I wondered why so people were patiently lining up in their cars. Are they offering customers free coffee? I picked up Justin.

M: Hey Justin, how is it going?

P: Not that well. Look around you. Everything is closing again. Look at all the stores down this strip mall that are closed. The bars and restaurants, even the theatre in town, are closed. Some places are reopening now, but it is still a big mess. Banks, Dollar stores, and a few adaptive fast-food restaurants are the only things left. The Dollar stores just announced they are raising prices to $1.25. Poor people will turn out in the streets to protest [Justin chuckles].

M: Still, a lot of other businesses are still open. I read every day that the economy is buzzing. Everyone is trying to adjust. I wonder who is making all the money?

P: Is that what you call it? Let me tell you what I have experienced over the last eighteen months. I have held four different jobs. None of them compared to my bartending job before the pandemic started.

P: I have been a bartender for half of my adult life. I made $82,000 last year working the bar. I endured many late nights, and it was very stressful. I spent all my free time in the gym working out, so I could handle the 65-hour per week schedule.

P: I worked 4:30 pm to 2:30 am shifts six days a week before the pandemic hit. Then the Covid-19 virus came in like a midwestern thunderstorm. It surprised me. So many got sick. They shut us down back in June of 2020. It took us about six weeks to complete the carry-out operation. Half of the staff either quit or disappeared during that period. I got laid off. I didn't know what to do. Then my dad got sick and almost died. He was bedridden for two months. I only had about $2500 in savings. That ran out quickly. There wasn't a restaurant or bar open around town in the summer of 2020, so I did some delivery work, you know, Door Dash and Grubhub food deliveries, to pay bills. It was not my thing.

P: My next position was as a fast-food restaurant manager. I will not tell you the specific one, but their main food products are hamburgers and chicken sandwiches. By Labor Day, I was desperate for cash. So, I took this management trainee post at a fast-food restaurant, hoping I would find something else once the bars and restaurants reopened.

P: Then they put me on the drive-thru window during training. The cars lined up all day. I worked ten hours often without a meal and got two restroom breaks. It was insane. The food orders were relentless. Oh, and odors [ha ha] drive us all batty. I don't know how these managers do it. I don't think they make a lot more than the employees. They work twice as many hours. It was a Mad Hatter experience. Who are all these crazy hungry people eating chicken sandwiches and French fries every damn day? I think the drive-thru was a terrible invention.

M: Perhaps you are right. Don't you think that drive-thrus saved the fast-food industry during the pandemic?

P: It may have saved the industry all right. It sure made working in that industry more difficult. Running the drive-thru, we are supposed to watch both screens. One camera views the customer; the other is where we type their food order. There are all these beeping sounds you hear in the headsets. Watch, and you can see managers working the kitchen AND taking drive-thru orders all at once! If there are two drive-thru lanes, each lane makes different beeping sounds. After a few days, I started hearing these beeping sounds in my sleep like an alarm clock was going off inside my head.

M: That doesn't sound healthy.

P: Here's the thing. We all know the drill. There are three times as many people now using the drive-thrus. Well, not all. Only the fast-food places have them because eating in your car remained a safe pandemic option. All the other dine-in options are gone.

M: I read that the entire drive-thru operation is on a 3-minute timer per customer. Any time measured over that from order-taking to delivery counts as a poorly managed order.

P: The company keeps track of this as you learn your manager-trainee role. Only the fastest and most accurate survive! If an order gets held up, managers will ask the customer to move to a waiting parking spot where they eventually bring your food to your car. If there was a long wait, such as breakfast items you can order at dinner time, or large orders, say, five or more special coffees, they would flag your performance report for that day. Customers are always getting angry. They cannot pay me enough for this crazy work. Plus, after working there, I will never eat their food again.

P: Yesterday, we had a lot of angry customers. In thirty minutes, we had a grill go down, one man ordered 30 meals for his soccer team, and two employees walked out because the manager [not me] kept yelling at them. If people wait for more than 5 minutes in the drive-thru, they know something must be wrong inside, and it is always the manager's fault. The drive-thru lineup is like a slow-boiling fire. People start exiting their cars, walking up to the window, swearing, and looking frustrated. Some leave and give me the finger as they drive off in a huff.

P: Seeing a long drive-thru lineup discourages most people from joining it, so the managers try their best to avoid stalled lines trying to slow the ordering process. You only have so many tools to work with here. They don't like it when you use managerial discretion. When someone orders 20 burger meals or two dozen chicken sandwiches, they should not call them in the drive-thru window line, which is supposed to provide fast service and effortless orders. I saw one manager go up to each car and try and explain the delays. It didn't go so well.

P: I also saw people pull into the dedicated parking spaces for drive-Thru pickup, and sit there instead of getting in line. You can see them trying to order through the app.

M: It seems like the pandemic overwhelmed fast food service. What didn't change were people's expectations.

P: The problem is that many people seem to lose their manners and politeness when entering a drive-thru. Politeness moved to the back of the line and disappeared when they got to those waiting parking spots. I think I quickly became part of the problem at our drive-thru. When people's orders were too large, I would tell them to pull into the parking lot and order online. We would have it ready faster. Some customers agreed, and others would argue with me.

P: A few waited a long time at the pick-up window, and you could see the people behind them getting mad. You see people arguing in their cars about what to do during a delay. They had already paid at the pay window and waited for what seemed like ages [only about ten minutes], yet they had nothing to do but wait

– I guess they wanted a drink - to show for their long wait. One guy asked for some free fries while he waited. I gave him some, and he said they were cold. I lasted two weeks, and then I quit. I don't see how people can do such a job. I imagine many people will be leaving their jobs during the pandemic period. It is just too damn hard.

I had to laugh to break the tension. We were still about 5 minutes from the destination [at a new job].

M: Where are you working now?

P: Oh, yeah, I am starting a new bartending job in Depot Town, Ypsilanti, tonight! I am excited because it is an excellent place owned by that company in town that owns about ten restaurants in Ann Arbor. I sure hope it works out. I am thankful for the work.

M: Me too. At least we are surviving this awful period. And I am thankful for the excellent story. It will surely make the Lyft book. It is an exciting tale, and I see you working at the drive-thru as part of the solution here. You seem to have kept your optimism alive throughout the ordeal.

P: Yeah, it has been a rough year. Hey, come by the bar someday. I'll buy YOU a drink.

M: Thanks, I will. I imagine we all could use one.

* * * * * * * * * * * *

The option to dine in disappeared in restaurants in 2021. People had to eat meals at home or in their cars. People that worked in bars and restaurants had to find new jobs. During the fall of 2021, food delivery and drive-thrus served as the primary [albeit expensive] solution for people to acquire meals.

Many businesses that shape our daily lives, such as restaurants, cafes, and grocery stores, adapted to the pandemic restrictions by reorganizing their operations and altering their ranks. As the Covid-19 pandemic spread in 2021, businesses had to pivot quickly to delivery and curbside service to survive. For example, drive-thrus and home delivery became the fast-food business' lifelines. More Ready-to-Eat food appeared at the grocery stores, and food delivery to people's homes grew dramatically.

Restaurants lost wait and cooking staff, while home delivery services like GrubHub and Door Dash expanded everywhere. Restaurants with drive-thru windows were suddenly swamped. These changes disrupted the entire labor force.

More people were eating in their cars out of concern for safety and convenience, especially during quarantine. Suddenly, fast-food businesses were booming and began offering higher wages to attract more low-end labor.

Even I ate in my car for the first time in 2021 and purchased a few drive-thru meals. I would not enjoy eating in my vehicle. The pandemic [along with Lyft driving] changed my daily routines profoundly. This passenger told me how his modes of travel and the mobility patterns changed too, less pedestrian, more costly, and less frequent.

This passenger said several times during our ride that he felt like a prisoner at his job. He lamented how tough his life [and work] had become. As a result, he endured several unwanted job changes and continued to experience serious challenges searching for some sense of normality. Managing a fast-food drive-thru is pressure-packed and relentless work, producing mental and physical fatigue and nervous anxiety that lasts for weeks. He believed that this kind of manager work was all he could find. I was troubled by my high level of fatigue and distressed feelings. I tried to remember the world before fast-food and drive-thrus.

Story Seven

Delivered to Your Door

October 3, 2021

"I started as a waiter, a door-to-door salesman, a car-washer, and a hotel doorman and moved right up to a food delivery boy. Man, I have done it all."

- Randeep Hooda

After ten days of Lyft driving in the Ypsilanti/Ann Arbor area, I started to see some passenger patterns. In addition, the rides themselves suggested circles and loops. I saw the many other delivery drivers on the road whom I usually take no notice of. My next ride started with a question from a young passenger.

M: Hello, welcome to my Lyft driving adventure. It looks like you have a package there by your front door.

P: Yeah, everything is being delivered to my front door. Do you think everything will be delivered to our homes in the future?

M: Geeze, I hope not. What a great question. The pandemic created the need to deliver many new things to people's homes. Have you seen the army of Amazon delivery vehicles on the roads? It is a scary and exciting time all at once. I have never felt so anxious about the future.

P: Yeah, I never thought I would be using a rideshare service like Lyft. I thought it was only for affluent people. My church did a fund-raiser for me and added $500 to my Lyft account.

M: Wow, that is great. So, I guess I will see more of you?

P: Do you like to Lyft drive?

M: Well, I can tell you what I like and don't like about Lyft driving. Lyft is for everyone as far as passengers go. Perhaps Lyft driving is not for everyone. What is strange is that I have yet to have a single direct conversation with another HUMAN BEING that works for Lyft. A profound thing for me to experience. After all, I am a professor of organizational behavior. I study how management functions, so I have my work cut out if I want to understand the new gig-work world.

P: Wow, that sounds amazing. Did you study all that as a Lyft driver?

M: Well, No, not exactly. I am retired now. I Lyft drive for something to do. It started to earn money to pay my bills. It is an unusual kind of employment arrangement. They call it gig work. I am learning how it works as I go. It is me, you, my car, and the app running the whole show. I turned Lyft driving into a professor job!

P: Yeah, so who is your boss?

M: I don't know, I am not sure. No one, I guess. Perhaps the app is my boss. Yet, I also supervise myself. I like that part, but I have been in a few situations where I could have used some human support. When things go wrong, I try my best to fix them. The Lyft application works quite well. But it is not perfect. I am unsure how they get usable feedback from us as drivers. Someday, I will talk to another Lyft driver or the company leaders. Then I can share my insights and concerns.

P: I had a job at Pizza Hut last year until they closed the place. They did not get enough carry out and the delivery services charged too much. They had three managers that controlled everything we did. I made pizzas and salads and filled orders for carry-out. I hated working there because the managers were always yelling at us. They yelled at us when we made mistakes and yelled at us when they needed our help. It was like living in a dysfunctional home. I got sick of it.

P: Then I got a job at Kohls. It was a lot better. The managers were more likable there. We always had a lot of contests and fantastic events. I had fun for the first time at work. Work is supposed to be social; you know?

M: What sort of events? They had pizza and ice cream parties and shopping sales just for the employees with as much as 35% off for like two hours before the store opened. Wow, that sounds fun.

P: Yes, the managers would dress up in Kohl's outfits and come and help you when things got busy. They never yelled at us. The place had a great atmosphere.

M: Maybe I should study Kohls next?

P: They also gave us money to go to college. I am the first one in my family to go to college! They told me I could be a manager in a year if I stayed on, but I am in college now. I am a freshman, she said proudly.

M: That is wonderful. I was the first in my own family to graduate from college. What do you want to study?

P: Philosophy! She said without any hesitation.

M: Really, that is an unusual choice. Why philosophy? Why not business or computer science?

P: Oh, that is what everyone is studying. Boring. I want to go eventually to Law School. My advisor said that philosophy would prepare me very well for law. That is the plan. I thought getting into law school was my only goal, but I had two philosophy courses this term. I loved them both.

P: Both of my professors told me that I am a natural. I like to read, and I work in the college library too. During the pandemic, I read many good books. My dad has a great library. He gave me this strange book at Christmas. that I still must read. It is called Riddley Walker. Have you heard of it?

M: Yes, I know it well. Riddley Walker by Russell Hoban is one of the most imaginative books ever written. I read it when I was about your age. Your father is a brilliant man. If he encourages you to read books like that, I should leave composing your future reading list to him.

P: We read books together sometime. I remember our first book called Sophie's World by Jostein Gaardner. Reading his book got me interested in philosophy. My dad and Mr. Gaardener are Norwegians. Did you enjoy being a professor?

M: Yes, I felt like I could not do anything else. Now, I am trying to figure out whether to retire or not, so I am writing a book about Lyft passenger stories and conversations.

P: Will our conversation be in your book?

M: Yes, it will. I recommend reading something that every serious beginning philosophy student reads early on. It is called the Allegory of the Cave by Plato.

P: Yeah, I know a little about Plato. My dad mentioned him. What is the title? Allegory of the Cave?

M: Yes, it is in Plato's book, The Republic, in either chapter seven or eight. You'll find it.

P: Thanks. I like reading philosophy because it challenges me to think. I wonder about all sorts of things. I have so many questions. Sometimes philosophy gives me some other answers, like church.

My minister always talks about God and Jesus and learning to be good. Do you ever get sick of hearing the same thing over and over?

M: In some ways, so did Plato. But the lesson of the allegory is how we live in a world of appearances. How we are subject to illusion and errors of perception that influence what we learn and know. The concept of what is [good] remains a mystery. Plato says that we can struggle to venture out of the dark cave of illusion and ignorance into the light of the good if we learn to remove our perceptual chains and see appearances for what they are shadows on the cave wall. Plato teaches us important ways to think.

P: Wow, thanks so much. I wrote it down. Here is my stop. Goodbye, Professor Brown. It was great meeting you.

M: Wonderful meeting you as well. Good luck with your philosophy studies.

****

At first, the prospect of having everything delivered to my front door seemed a luxury for the wealthy. We talked about the recent emergence of the affordable delivery services that people call [gig work], yet this young passenger had an unusual view of work. I shared with her some of my experiences as a Lyft driver, and she taught me about the value service work provides and why we pay for it.

Everyone I picked up unloaded their gripes about work, vented about their life's mishaps and complained about personal struggles or how horrible the pandemic treated them. This ride was unique. It was the most fun ride I had had so far.

A wounded soldier had his moment of good cheer and optimism despite his overwhelming physical and mental challenges. An older woman helped me discover my deeper empathy; yet this young woman reminded me how terrific life can be at twenty years old.

She was so full of the pure enthusiasm of youth, optimistic about the future, hungry for knowledge, questioning everything, and inspired by reading some of the classics of literature as I was. I was thrilled to have met a young, budding scholar carrying the torch of academic learning. She was as genuine, thoughtful questioner as I was back in the days of my youth.

She gave me a gift of remembrance and renewed my interest in studying philosophy and literature, weighing and considering the [big why] questions. So much of what we attend to in the modern media world is trash.

How about that, I thought. Here is a young woman who appears to break the mold; no software engineering or computer science for her. She wants to learn more about human ideas.

First, she signed up for college because her parents were lawyers and told her that majoring in philosophy was the best way to get into law school; she took her introduction to philosophy course and got hooked on the subject. I gave her a few pointers, some references to authors she might investigate, and even the title of one of my favorites. I wished I could have done more for her, but I am a Lyft driver!

Story Eight

Willow Run

October 4, 2021

"I probably wouldn't be a good spokesman for an electric car because I'll still get on a private jet, and one flight on a private plane undoes all my electric-car good deeds."

-George Clooney

I started driving later than usual on Monday at 3:00. I needed a rest from the first six days of driving and writing. During my first seven days of Lyft driving, I collected eight stories. However, on Day Eight, I clocked five hours of driving without securing a single compelling tale. By ten past eight, it started getting dark. Suddenly, a ride request flashed on my screen. I was so tired I almost missed it. I decided to extend my strict schedule Drive for Five to consider one last ride request before heading home because the pick-up was at the Willow Run Airport.

Willow Run is the name of the regional airport two miles east of Ypsilanti, MI. I thought this late ride might provide a rare opportunity to hear an unusual story. It is a smaller regional airport between Ypsilanti and the larger Detroit Wayne Metropolitan Airport to the east. I had never been to the airport before.

I was unfamiliar with the airport landscape and had trouble finding the passenger terminal. There were no streetlights, no signal lights or signs. I circled a few non-descript buildings and saw a couple emerge. I pulled up, and they got into the car silently. He immediately answered a phone call. I thought they were executives busy typing away on their phones. They didn't talk to each other but seemed to be communicating by looks and smiles.

P: Are you familiar with where Grosse Pointe is?

M: Yes, I said. I grew up near there in Detroit.

I told them I grew up in Detroit, approximately one mile from their destination. They asked me how I became a Lyft driver. I told them I was a semi-retired professor working on a book about passenger stories. That was their cue to tell me a story.

P: OK, we can share our story. First, you might wonder why we flew into Willow Run Airport." My company owns a private jet, and we fly quite a lot. We usually fly into other private airports partly to avoid the commercial traffic at DTW. We provide added luxury [and privacy] to our preferred clients.

M: What do you do?

P: I am an executive in the auto industry. My wife is a consultant. We are back from a conference for auto dealership owners in Los Angeles. Next, we meet with all our Detroit Area dealers to discuss information from the national convention. Auto dealerships are facing some big decisions.

M: How so?

P2: I can give you a general example. Do you know how everything we purchase these days is delivered straight to our homes? Automobile service, like everything else, will be provided at your home. This trend is affecting the entire automobile industry as it moves toward electrification.

P2: I am a market strategist in the auto industry. The automobile business is changing rapidly, and the old dealership business model won't work in the electric future. They are learning that their "big box" retail car "selling and servicing" model is too costly and obsolete.

P2: The only area they make real money is in auto service. About 70% of a dealership's revenue is servicing vehicles. Most people think they make money from selling new cars. During the talk at this auto dealer conference, my wife asked the audience of dealership owners, how are you going to bring auto service to your next customer's doorstep? She also said, "Consider when electric cars begin to dominate the product lines you now sell. Those cars don't need the same mechanical and maintenance services that gas-powered vehicles need. Are you fully ready for the transformation?

M: I know a little about electric cars. The engines and drivetrains are entirely different, no more oil changes, no more exhaust repairs, no more fuel-line freezes. You are going to need more battery techs and software engineers. Sure, the cars will still have tires, drivetrains, seats, and steering wheels, but everything about vehicles will change, and you need to understand these changes if you want to survive in this business.

P2: It is a bit scary to listen to because my words can seem like the harbinger of doom. Yet, sounding the alarm and waking people up that have become wealthy and complacent is part of the message. Some want them to get ahead of the pandemic upheaval. Others are learning to adapt quickly.

M: Wow, that sounds like exciting work. Do you think the big motor mall car dealerships will all soon disappear?

P2: Well, they will transform or will likely vanish as shopping malls did in the 1990s. Nissan is re-purposing their Japanese dealerships into "Experience Centers" where potential customers can test out new vehicles but learn about the new car maintenance at the home experience from end to end and without ANY sales pressure.

P: Salespeople have always been educators and customer relationship builders. They have changed their approach to winning customers by trying to be the best automotive transportation educators. They even teach people about rideshare and Lyft.

M: I read about car manufacturing companies working with companies like Salesforce, Amazon, and even Lyft to reimagine the public transportation industry. I can imagine them starting to offer incentives to Lyft drivers using electric vehicles.

P: It is an exciting time. You said you were a business professor?

M: I taught organizational behavior and strategic management for twenty years.

P: Well, this all should come as no real surprise. My industry is all about two things: mobility and innovation. Well, yes, and the customers too.

M: To move people around in new ways, we may have to meet them first at their front door. That is where everything will be delivered!

P: That's a clever way to put it.

P: Well, that is my wife's alarm ringing. We must get on this call. My boss, GM CEO Mary Barra, is speaking. She knows what is coming. GM has a once-in-a-generation opportunity here.

M: I sure hope GM stays here in Michigan…I don't see the departure like what happened in the 1980s. Cities like Detroit and Flint suffered huge population and tax revenue losses.

M: Yes, I think there is broad mutual interest in not repeating that part of history.

P: We all know that EVs are coming in strong in the next couple of years. We have much work to catch Tesla's head start. I think Cadillac will lead the GM charge. Our new electrics will lead the way.

M: I wonder if Lyft drivers can afford the new EVs?

P: Sure, why not?

M: You two just flew in on a private plane. You live in Grosse Pointe and take a Lyft ride home. I wonder why you don't drive your vehicle to the airport.

P: Yes, I guess you could say we are well off, yet we frugal and try to save where we can, as most folks do. We have two kids in college and a sizable mortgage. We aren't rich by any means, but very comfortable. I count my blessings every day.

P: You said you were a retired professor. I imagine you made a handsome salary. I bet you will be in the market for an electric car next year.

M: Perhaps, I would love to have my first new vehicle be an electric car.

P: Well, here is my card. If you decide to consider buying or leasing a Cadillac, drop me a line, and I will recommend someone you can trust, someone that knows how to build a relationship and not merely sell you a car.

M: I might have to find another line of work besides Lyft driving. This book project grew into my second job! I was about to retire.

P: Well, it is a great idea. I look forward to reading it. It was a pleasure to meet you, Matthew. Here is our house right on the left. Thanks.

****

GPS usually locates passengers for pick up accurately. Yet on occasion, a general address was provided, and then I had to search around to find my customers. Then as I circled what I thought was an airplane hangar, a well-dressed man and woman emerged from an unmarked metal door. There did not seem to be a recognizable terminal entrance or exit.

Most of my Lyft passengers were working-class folks and local college students. These two passengers were different. Like the Parent's Weekend crowd and Foodie groups, these outlier passengers provided a window to observe Lyft customers that were executives.

It was refreshing and surprising to serve passengers: one a business executive and the other a consultant. Their daily experiences included private plane travel, convention keynote speaking, and executive advising. I was curious to learn why they chose to use Lyft and what kinds of work they did.

I picked them up at Willow Run Airport, historically an essential part of wartime airplane production during WWII. Its factories were part of Ford Motor Company, the automobile company that invented the assembly line that enabled mass production. At its height, Willow Run was a vast industrial manufacturing facility of 64 acres that produced several thousand B-24 bombers. Every 62 minutes, a finished B-24 bomber rolled off the assembly line at Willow Run in 1942.

They were a handsome couple and younger than me. When we arrived at their home, it was a multimillion-dollar property located in one of the wealthiest corners of Grosse Pointe, where the old money of Detroit resides.

I told them I was a retired professor of organizational behavior, currently writing a book, and collecting passenger stories, and their attitude toward me improved. I began testing this out on later passengers. It proved an effective conversation starter.

I still didn't feel I got an answer to why they took Lyft rides to the airport. Perhaps the reason to procure a Lyft ride was that it was easier to do, and they didn't have to worry about where to park, drive, or pay attention. They could easily afford the service, which was cheaper than a limousine. It was that simple.

Story Nine

Airbnb and New Lodging

October 5, 2021

"Airbnb has proven that hospitality, generosity, and the simple act of trust between strangers can go a long way."

-Joe Gebbia

I began to wonder how Lyft was like Airbnb. If you think about it, they are both platforms connecting customers with a specific service. The services they deliver are connected. Lyft provides a ride in a vehicle directly from point to point. Airbnb is the other way to book a stay [destination] where that destination can be a private citizen willing to lodge guests at their homes overnight for a fee. My next passenger's name was Ted.

M: Where to Ted?

P: We're going to my second home in Ann Arbor. My mother's old home.

M: OK, sounds great.

P: Yeah, I inherited a big old house a few years ago. Last year, I turned it into an Airbnb. It has five bedrooms and is close [walking distance] to the UM main campus. My daughter runs the entire show there.

M: Wow, I don't know much about Airbnb. Tell me more. Tell me about your innovating and redesigning the rooms your rent out.

P: The best thing about this house is its four bathrooms, making the bedrooms self-contained. But I had to get a completely new on-demand hot water system first. My daughter's room is the only bedroom on the first floor. We figured it out. There are flexible accommodations from one person to a family of eight [ten with two extra cots]. Once, a considerable family came for two nights and rented all the rooms.

P: The significant innovation happened when we redecorated the rooms and started matching room rentals to people's diverse tastes and needs.

One of the first things I did was make the house disabled-friendly by getting a mobile stair-lift machine and refitting one of the bathrooms to be more handicapped accessible. It cost me about $5000, but I figured the special needs elements were worth the investment. It was. It turned out to be an excellent idea. People with anything from a single room to an entire mansion can list their property for rent using the Airbnb service. Airbnb's website and app allow people looking for a place to stay in a particular location to sort through those listings to find something that meets their needs.

M: You can often stay at an Airbnb with more space and amenities than a hotel room at a significantly lower cost. I went to the local hotels and investigated their prices, which changed with the seasonal demand. Rooms during a football weekend go for over $200 a night. I charge half that much.

P: The goal is to get to 100% occupancy on any day, but I would settle for 80-85%. The biggest hurdle to doing this is the legal part. Some cities have laws restricting your ability to host paying guests for short periods. These laws are often part of a city's zoning or administrative codes. In some cities, you must register, get a permit, or obtain a license before listing your property on Airbnb. That is the case here. Certain types of short-term bookings may be prohibited altogether."

It is tricky. Dedicated short-term rental properties such as Airbnb houses that aren't owner-occupied are not allowed in residential neighborhoods. So, that means you can only run an Airbnb if you occupy the home [which my daughter does].

The A2 City Council passed an ordinance in 2020 that banned short-term rentals in residential districts, including Airbnbs. However, the law still permitted some Airbnbs and other short-term rentals in mixed-use — meaning both commercial and residential — zoning districts in residential districts if the property was owner-occupied while also being rented. My home is in the mixed-use zone.

P: In many ways, it is a hotel without many extra hotel costs. I just wanted people coming to the UM campus for short periods to have another option. There is a shortage of accessible lodging within walking distance of the campus. That is my competitive advantage.

M: It is simply supplying people with an unmet customer need. He is a businessman. That is how entrepreneurship works. You fulfill an unmet need for people willing to pay. I thought of Lyft. The rideshare innovation is like Airbnb. It is part of this thing we call the sharing economy. It turns out that a little extra trust can be of great value. With rideshare, the customer trusts a stranger to drive them safely to a destination for an acceptable price. That driver drives their car and assumes most liability for driving passengers. Airbnb customers trust homeowners that share unoccupied rooms for short-term stays for a fair price. I see that these two businesses are very similar.

M: What makes it all possible beyond the trust of strangers is the technology platforms that are programmed to match up customers with providers. The Airbnb platform reconciles both sides of any transaction. The platform works very well. You get paid for every rental room you deliver for Airbnb, don't you? Is Lyft a good fit for you?

M: Yeah, it works OK. It may not be a career-type job, but Lyft driving sure came in handy when I wasn't earning any income.

P: I don't know if I would be doing this had I not inherited this house. A sorority wanted to buy it from me. Then a child-care company approached me with an offer. I would have sold the property had Airbnb not come along. It's a perfect fit for me. My Airbnb is a housing option for visitors to the Ann Arbor area, and those visitors deserve to have these options available.

Over the last year, we've had several entire families visit who've had to come to the University hospital and quarantined for several days before being admitted for holidays with family members. It is hard to do that in a hotel.

****

Listening to passengers, I discovered how Lyft and Airbnb were similar in operation and user experience. Rideshare has revolutionized public transportation making it an affordable and a point-to-point service delivered by independent owner/drivers. Airbnb has changed the hotel/lodging landscape by turning homes into affordable hotels [Bed and Breakfast].

My passenger inherited a house in Ann Arbor close to the University. His new lodging business is essentially people visiting the University of Michigan looking for a "proximity to campus" deal that competes with the hotels in the area. Airbnb also offers people lodging flexibility while in transition moving to a new location. For example, later that same day, I drove a young family home from the airport to their Ann Arbor Airbnb. They were from Iran. The father was an engineering post-doc, and the mother was a medical physicist starting her job working at the University of Michigan hospital. They told me Airbnb made it possible for them to immigrate from Canada after the newborn's mother was offered a hospital position.

Airbnb works well for people moving to new areas offering a longer-term rental option that is more affordable than an extended hotel-motel stay. Airbnb keeps hotel prices down and is especially attractive to people looking for lodging during university events.

UM and EMU students needing short-term rental during the COVID-19 spring 2021 spike often used Airbnb to find quarantine space outside of the Universities' facilities. One freshman stayed in a local Airbnb with her parents after being exposed to COVID-19 in the residence halls. She said the Airbnb experience was beneficial to her mental health and productivity as she navigated 14 days of isolation.

I had many more questions about how Airbnb works. Like Lyft driving, running an Airbnb home requires a high degree of trust. My passenger told me that in some venues, people rent Airbnbs to have parties increasing the risks and liabilities for Airbnb owners who are now starting to reject guest stays intended for purposes other than typical overnight stays and those without a positive rental record. I thought of how as a Lyft driver, I sometimes reject passenger rides I deem unsafe.

Story Ten

Meet Your New Boss

October 6, 2021

Humans invent technology. Technology enables human labor and management. Wherever technology can replace human labor and management, it will.

Now that I am driving to earn money, I am fascinated by the Lyft driver application. I do not think of it as my manager. I prefer to think of it as my quiet, not-so-humble driving assistant. However, I am learning that the Lyft application silently controls much of what I do as a driver. During the next few weeks, I hope to better understand how it works and how I am being manipulated.

M: Hi Omar, where are we headed?

P: Center for Creative Studies in Detroit.

M: That is a bit outside my driving territory, but I know where it is. Are you a student there?

P: Yeah, I am visiting a friend in Ann Arbor. He graduated last year as a computer scientist. He creates algorithms that run facial recognition software for the FBI and other police agencies. He is torn a little by what he does for law enforcement agencies. We argue about the uses of these algorithms. These programs are not perfectly accurate. There have been life-changing consequences because of algorithms, too, particularly in the hands of the police.

M: Accurate face recognition must be impossible with everyone wearing masks?

M: I know, for instance, that several Black and Asian men, at least, recently have been wrongfully arrested due to the use of these facial-recognition systems. They are used widely in Asian countries such as China and Korea.

P: There's often little more than a basic explanation from tech companies on how these algorithmic systems work. I am lucky because I can pick my friend's brains and learn how they work.

M: Should we fear what is coming?

P: Beyond that, experts like my friend tell me that the technology is still flawed, and tech surveillance laws are useless and way behind their use. We call them black boxes. Computer-based management and platforms employing this technology for security are inside the black box, which means we don't know how they work. Those who build these systems don't always know why/how they reach conclusions.

M: Computer scientists and data scientists, at this current stage, seem like wizards to most people because they don't understand what they do. We think they always know, and that's not always the case. Algorithms, can you explain what they are exactly? Are they the same as programs?

P: At their most basic, an algorithm is a series of instructions that can be hard-coded, with fixed directions for a computer to follow, such as to put a list of names in alphabetical order or soft-coded to adapt to a variety of input choices that shift the programming path as new information becomes available. Simple algorithms used for computer-based decision-making have been around for decades.

Today's algorithms are much more sophisticated programs. They facilitate otherwise-complicated processes, whether we know it or not. They are working in the background, often vast amounts of data to remote host computers.

M: So, when we direct a clothing website to filter pajamas to see the most popular or least expensive options, you're using an algorithm essentially to say, "Hey, Old Navy, go through the steps to show me the cheapest jammies."

P: A recipe, for instance, is a sort of algorithm, as is the weekday morning routine you sleepily shuffle through before leaving the house.

P: We all run on our algorithms every day. We are correcting the code to produce a prescribed range of solutions most of the time. While we can challenge and interrogate our own decisions, those made by machines have become increasingly enigmatic and difficult to unpack. The rise of a form of AI known as deep learning modeled after the way neurons work in the brain has now gained prominence. It started about a decade ago.

P: There are now deep-learning algorithms that might task a computer to look at thousands of videos of cats, for instance, and then it learns to identify a cat. (It was a big deal when Google figured out how to do this reliably in 2012.) They call it data "bingeing" and the algorithm improves the result over time. In essence, a computer-generated procedure for how the computer will identify whether there is a cat in any new pictures—is known as an algorithm.

M: I know these programs can be incredibly complex and need other platforms to run them. Facebook, Salesforce, Instagram, and Twitter all use them to help personalize users' feeds based on each person's interests and prior activity (oh, and track our internet use).

M: Yeah, it is that last part that worries me. I can imagine these algorithms being used to track Lyft drivers. On the plus side, it might help us optimize our earnings. On the negative side, it could be a new form of surveilance and invasion of privacy.

P: What do you think of algorithms tracking everyone's movements?

P: The amount of data is huge. No one could process it all even with an advanced system. The models can store data collected over many years that no human could ever sort through. For instance, Zillow was using its trademarked, machine-learning assisted "Zestimate" to estimate the value of homes since 2006, considering tax and property records and homeowner-submitted details such as the addition of a bathroom and pictures of a house. It was overwhelming.

M: One of the most dangerous things about Lyft driving. You pick up a passenger. They have requested a ride to a very sketchy part of town. Now, I grew up in Detroit. I don't go into some crime-ridden regions because I know better. I am alone and a white male over 65. It is not about race, but you never want to put yourself in a highly vulnerable circumstance where certain people harbor criminal intentions.

M: I drop off a passenger at the destination. A ride request can originate from any physical address. I receive a ride request from a location nearby. Yet, on rare occasions, that ride request has me picking someone up at an abandoned house. If that happens, I cannot afford to waste time checking out the dwelling or waiting for the passenger to show up. I need to leave and cancel the request for my safety. The algorithms matching ride requests with available drivers do not know the potential danger in such circumstances. You must assess the risk yourself.

P: As Zillow's case shows, however, offloading decision-making to algorithmic systems can also go awry in excruciating ways, and it's not always clear why. Zillow recently decided to shutter its home-flipping business, Zillow Offers, showing how hard it is to use AI to value real estate.

In February of 2021, the Zillow company said its "Zestimate" would represent an initial cash offer from the company to purchase the property through its house flipping business. By November, the company took a $304 million inventory write-down. It blamed losses on having recently purchased homes for prices higher than it thinks it can sell them. The real reason might have been Zestimate meltdown.

Zillow's home-buying debacle shows us how difficult it is to use AI to value real estate. Elsewhere online, Meta, the company formerly known as Facebook, has come under scrutiny for tweaking its algorithms in a way that helped incentivize more negative content on the world's largest social network. We may see Meta move all the harmful content to its Metaverse.

****

As a professor of management and organization, I have a lingering question: Do rideshare and Airbnb platforms signal the widespread disappearance of management? Disappearance may be the key term. Intelligent programs and algorithms such as Lyft and Airbnb push management into the background. It only seems to disappear because oversight functioning runs underneath what we see and do. The real issue is how can we make sense of management activity and its purposes if we cannot interact and access management information?

As a Lyft driver [employee], its management functions are embedded in its digital technology. I have no direct contact with any other Lyft managers or employees, including the company leadership. I argue that this changes the social contract of work in fundamental ways. My new supervision [or manager] is a computer application. I am not sure how I feel about this. For example, I don't know how ride requests work. I enjoy the bonus and streak-earning opportunities, yet I also view them as managerial enticements to drive more.

Independent work is about choice, discretion, and control. We all want more of each of these, so we don't feel oppressed and restricted in doing our job. When I began Lyft driving, I assumed that the rides available to me were simply chosen by location – however, I now find it is a delicate matching process where price, location, and ride length are only partial factors in determining ride availability. I may never know how it works, but Lyft has hundreds of data scientist at work doing what exactly is anyone's guess. I know one thing, there is huge value in the dataset being generated by rideshare.

I can afford to keep things simple. Drivers go online and accept the Lyft rides offered. If I take the ride requests that the Lyft Driver app provides me and deliver a safe and pleasant ride to a destination, then the passenger is satisfied and the Lyft app does the rest. Simple. Or is it?

Something about how the Lyft application works sparks my deeper curiosity: I can't fathom how the programming works underneath what I see and do. I can't make sense of it because I have no access to it as I would have with another human being. All I have is my imagination and my inheent skepticism. It is impossible to completely understand how any Lyft algorithm works without considering its intentions and by interviewing/interogating software programmers that write the code. I wonder how the real asset created by Lyft [the database] with its treasure trove of passengers and ride-tracking data will be used.

I imagine that as the driver and passenger information database evolves, so will it yield new ways of organizing public/private transportation rather than simply adding more advertising noise and the further commercialization of all human knowledge- a great temptation today.

Story Eleven

Call Center Blues

October 7, 2021

"If a factory is torn down but the rationality which produced it is left standing, then that rationality will simply produce another factory. If a revolution destroys a government, but the systematic patterns of thought that produced that government are left in tact, then those patterns will repeat themselves...there is so much talk about the system. And so little understanding."

- Robert Pirsig, Zen and the Art of Motorcycle Maintenance

Something strange is happening in the workforce these days. So many Lyft passengers were facing the decision to switch to work at home or remain working at a plant or office. It was a voluntary or recommended choice and a company mandate for others. The choice sometimes hinged on whether they had access to affordable and convenient transportation. This passenger taught me how flexibility influenced the work choices about when/where to work and the challenges of other daily life decisions.

P: I have always wanted to work from home, so I applied to work at a call center for the Home Style Warehouse (HSW - disguised name). I figured that because I don't have a car. I cannot take the bus to work and consistently be on time. I didn't want to spend $35 daily for Lyft rides to work. Working at home would be safer and cheaper. I have close friends that suffered from the Covid-19 virus. I don't want my babies to get sick.

P: Quite frankly, I was glad this was an option because I needed the money. So, I joined the call center and began answering calls from disgruntled customers for Home Style Warehouse (HSW). When the pandemic started back in early March of 2020. I found out from a friend how to work from home. She told me about a company that would hire me to work in their call center and use my phone.

P: I decided to try it out. The company was called Sunshine Call Services (SCS - pseudonym). I had to complete (and pay for) the call center training to become fully hired. I was on probation until I finished it. It cost me $450, and they deducted it from my pay during the first three months. Then they asked me if I wanted to train in sales, customer service, or other types of customer support? Did I feel comfortable communicating with customers via chat or email?

P: I chose customer service because it seemed more closely related to my experience in retail. I want to tell you a story. I cannot prove it, but I believe racism at work is a problem in the call center business. It goes like this. Can you believe that people think they can tell the color of a person just by talking over the phone? Maybe so, but do you think a computer program can do this? So, imagine that you are a black person calling in. Your call can be re-routed to a customer service person who is also black. Why would they do that?

M: I don't know. Why do you think they would?

P: Is it because someone thought I might be able to resolve the issues of black customers better than white ones? That is racist. At first, I didn't think about it much, but then as I got to know some other call center associates through social media, I got angry.

P: Is this even legal? So, I began to ask about it. People stopped talking to me at work. I felt that it was at least a discriminatory policy. The manager said that the algorithms that route customer calls do NOT discriminate by race or anything else. However, you may be assigned a particular geographical area where the race or ethnicity of the callers may be slightly skewed toward or representing more of one group or another.

M: Hmmm. I thought that sounded like a strange management

response.

P: Then I met this other call center employee on social media that was also black, but she was from Jamaica and had a slight British accent. Were calls routed to her because of her color or ethnicity? The manager said her voicing was sophisticated. She had a delightful voice and knew the script. She seemed bothered. The manager then said that she had the highest performance numbers in her group, which was our group. I knew something was wrong because I was among the lowest performers.

P: Two significant factors determined our performance: the first was the speed of resolving your customer calls. Speed scores were proportionate to how complex the problem was [1-5] and how irritated the customer was [1-5]. Two was the number of customer resolutions [and supervisor escalations] charted in one shift of ten hours. It was best to minimize escalations because too many would make you appear incompetent or slow.

P: I told my friend that customers would call and immediately yell at me. That made it almost impossible for me to help resolve their issue. I had to escalate many of these calls to my supervisors. That made my performance numbers fall. My friend said that no one seemed to ever yell at her about their issues remaining polite after speaking with them for just a few minutes.

P: I was reprimanded twice for escalating too many calls to the supervisors. The company training videos told us that the call centers use a precise and effective escalation process to help customer service handle difficult calls.

P: I remembered the video said, "If a customer becomes irate or disrespectful, we ask the customer service associate to have their supervisor take over the call or transfer the call to the resolution queue." They seem to have this way of dealing with angry customers by putting them in a call queue. It is kind of like being put on hold forever.

P: If we used this process, we were not supposed to be penalized. I got to a point where I only used it in the very worst cases, maybe once a day. Sunshine Call policy and processes included the ability to disconnect callers without penalty or transfer these calls to support resources if they cannot de-escalate the situation. Sunshine Call does not tolerate discrimination or harassment of any kind," the statement said.

P: Then I was transferred to sales. Sales calls are challenging because I did cold calls. I lasted six weeks, and then I was let go for not making my sales numbers! The final insult was when they sent me a bill for the remaining training sessions!

P: Have you ever worked for a call center?

M: Only once. At the University, they get students to call alumni and ask for donations. You had to learn this script, but it was easy to do. Well, sometimes it was pleasant. Most people were OK. They didn't get mad. Yet when a rude or angry customer loses their cool, it becomes a nightmare.

P: Do Lyft passengers get mad at you?

M: Yeah, whenever someone gets in my car carrying some anger. They may displace it on me. I try and diffuse it. Sometimes they get angry if I miss a turn because they think I am not paying attention. I listen to their stories, and the GPS is occasionally too slow or in error. It hasn't happened very many times. Yet, avoid anything that annoys passengers.

P: My call center work made me wonder if working at home was healthier. I like to talk on the phone. I do it all the time. However, when it was my job, I started to hate it. Sometimes, I wanted to throw my phone in the trash, but I paid $750 [about what I make in a good week as a Lyft Driver].

****

Taking the center manager job was demoralizing to this passenger. He desperately wanted to go back to being a bartender or server. That job held a better kind of social interaction. Call Center work gave him little satisfaction, making him feel powerless— At least one gets tips as a bartender when the customers feel you have provided them good service was the joke.

The large percentages of people performing service work require little education or training. The result is that human work remains dull yet closely supervised. Many complained that employee training and supervision had become scripted and rigid, making their jobs unbearable and boring. They complained of receiving no benefits. I am increasingly interested in how people feel about their new managers and the changing nature of their work under platform-based supervision.

Interestingly, society has become so complex that we need legions of service personnel to facilitate daily economic and social transactions. I read in Forbes magazine that 85% of all businesses in America perform some service function today. Only 13% of enterprises manufacture or produce anything physical. That is the opposite distribution of business types and employee roles in the 1960s.

During the pandemic upheaval, I observed people becoming increasingly unsatisfied with their employment and work conditions. More and more passengers expressed extreme distress in their jobs. This condition was particularly acute in the low-end labor service areas such as fast-food, retail, and warehouse distribution. People told me they were "jumping" to other jobs that paid one dollar an hour more.

The situation was alarming. I learned first-hand about the volatility of low-end labor markets in the US. High turnover caused many employers to recreate jobs with even more efficient, less costly training and supervision. To put it bluntly, many people lost their jobs due to the pandemic. Yet, interestingly they were also quitting their jobs in amazingly high numbers to move to better pay and hopefully more fulfilling work.

Lyft has created some clever enticements for drivers such as streaks and bonuses designed to get you to drive/earn more with Lyft. It is short-term motivation to do more driving, a relatively tame form of managerial influence. It is difficult to live a good life working these low-paying jobs. They help you survive, but not much more. The story collecting is what kept me Lyft driving.

Story Twelve

Amazonians

October 8, 2021

The storyteller is the new assembly-line worker of the 21st century. The setting is the world of manual labor, a semi-automated warehouse distribution center. However, their role doesn't involve manufacturing any product. They move various products from place to place, the service distribution of billions of everyday goods. It was early in the morning, around 5:30 am. The first time I picked someone up working in the Amazon distribution center, I went to the wrong entry. These massive warehouses were the size of seven football fields and located in the middle of large lots surrounding the DTW airport.

P: Three years ago, I took a job as an Amazonian warehouse picker. When they first hired me, I watched several boring videos about working at Amazon for two days. I used to work at Boise Cascade as an order filler in one of their warehouses, but this job pays better. I work in this vast warehouse building. It has four floors and lots of noisy conveyors and robots. It is about the size of eight football fields and does not have very many windows. I never know what the weather is like outside. It is always a little chilly in here. I think that is intentional. I was taken to my first workstation and immediately learned the item-picking process.

P: The manager hovered around my station during that first day. I know he was checking on me. He did answer some of my questions. Then the manager picked items for about ten minutes so I could watch.

M: It must be unnerving to have someone looking over your shoulder while learning how to do the work.

P: Yeah, they made me nervous, but they were there during the first few days, maybe for the first week. Then I hardly saw a manager around at all unless something went wrong. I worked at what Amazon calls an ARSAW sorting station with conveyors to remove the crates/boxes we fill with the picked items. We refer to the plastic product bins as "totes."

P: These robots carry pods to your station. The pods are six-foot-high cubes with products in the stackable bins. The robots ride under the pods and move them around the warehouse. They seem to be programmed to go to different stations based on the orders that show up on our computer screens.

M: It must be cool watching hundreds of robots moving the pods around like little beetles or ants scurrying across the warehouse floor in all directions. They never stop or get tired.

P: Separated into two areas, the warehouse divides humans from the robots. The robot/pods stay on their side of the building.

P: The picker stations form a perimeter around the pod-carrying robots. I Never, never step foot in robot territory. If you do, you will get fired.

P: A computer screen in front of you displays the item. The screen displays a picture of the item, and below is a written description. It also tells you where in the pod it is likely to be. Only one side of the pod faces the workstation when parking alongside. Each bin slot is lettered and numbered. You must skim it. Most of the time, it is only 1 item to be picked.

P: When I pick an item from the bin, I scan its barcode under the light beam. If it's the correct item, I will hear a positive beep. If it's not the correct item, I will listen to a different sound and begin a new search for the right item. I do this for ten hours with two 20-minute breaks and a half-hour unpaid lunch: ten and a half-hour shifts, four days a week.

P: Amazonian wants you to work fast and then go more quickly. The managers your Takt time, and I asked them what Takt stands for. Takt simply means the number of operations [products picked correctly] over the time [any given interval] to measure performing a task. An example of a Takt measure would be six correct picks per minute. However, you can not stop working and pause the clock while measuring Takt.

P: We can only do that when we must go to the restroom or when managers and technicians go and fix a minor conveyor issue. I can pick around three thousand items on a good day during a 10-hour shift. An average picking time for one item (my Takt time) is around 9 seconds. That means 275-375 items an hour. I am sure the Amazonian managers would love it to be 8 1/2 seconds.

M: Interesting. We talk about learning how Takt time is used in my operations management course. I can see how this simple measure is still valuable for today's warehouse managers. It produces a stressful work environment though. It is disturbing they rely on Takt because this measure emphasizes only speed. There is a long and problematic history of using such work performance measures. They wee invented and commonly used a hundred years ago. You would think a company like Amazon could come up with better management tools.

P: They try to make it a game by putting the best Takt times on a giant board. I think they want us to compete. Can you imagine competing for the fastest time? Some people do. Trying to find specific items in the bin can take 3 seconds. Sometimes longer.

P: I get frustrated if I can't immediately find an item in the bin. Learning when and when not to read some item descriptions is the key to going fast.

P: I look at the monitor as quickly as I can. I can recognize the product from the picture, so I know what I am looking for without reading the description. Roughly 50% of the time, I'll know what I am to match from the picture. Other times I must read part of the description as well. And other times, I will read most of the item descriptions. But that is when I think I am wasting time. Sometimes I try and make my work a game I am playing, but it doesn't work for long. I feel so anxious doing this type of work. It is like having someone looking over your shoulder while you play poker.

M: Do you think there is a better way to do it? How about making it a kind of game?

P: Thinking of what I am doing is like playing a game makes it easier sometimes. But it doesn't last, and then I feel so mentally exhausted after a couple of days of working 10 hours a day, four days in a row. We get a premium wage to work in hell. Hey! Free donuts.

P: They have this schedule you can request called the donut shift, which is having a day off after two days of work, then you work two more shifts followed by two more days off. You might think that working four straight nights followed by three nights off sounds good, right? It's not that much better. I would be happier working five days with 8-hour shifts.

M: Also, if you don't get a good night's sleep (so many work nights, so they sleep during the day), you will regret it every time. I drive for five hours a day and sleep about ten hours!

P: What is weird is that I always feel like I am about to find an item, and it annoys me to pause and look at the monitor to read a full paragraph description to confirm it is the correct pick. Then I toss or place the item in the tote bin and touch the blinking green light, and that completes that one picking and look up at the monitor to determine the next item. It is monotonous, and that is what tires me out. Once you get worn out, you don't seem to recover for a long time.

M: The same thing happens to me when I drive too much. What happens when the totes fill up? Do you then push them down the conveyor with an empty tote? I imagine doing this makes you feel some relief rather than accomplishment.

P: I wanted it to end. Sad, huh? There is so much bending, squatting, and lifting to place and replace totes. Watching your Takt time goes higher. There is no relief. They sure figured out how to work us into the ground here.

P: I find myself muttering swear words. I never used to do that. When something goes wrong, I get mad. I get angry more than I did before I started this work. I still have two more hours and thirty minutes until the end of my shift. I am going to need counseling. Others drink or smoke marijuana when they get off work. You choose what intoxication club to join. Sometimes, I stop working for a quick minute, take a sip of water, and guess what? I look at the clock again. I mean, that's the only reality check available. You can't look at your phone, or you will get reprimanded by a floor manager. It is a bit like a prison, you know, no one to talk to and cameras watching your every move.

M: There are many people that share that. I hear a lot of stories where people describe work like being in prison.

P: You look at how much time you've spent picking on this quarter shift (each shift has two breaks and 20-minute lunch), and you figure your count per quarter and by the hour. The total of items picked for a one-quarter session is posted on your monitor and comes up on the game monitor for everyone to see. I want to know what my item picking rate is per hour.

P: Easy Peezy, Lemon Squeezy! Every 20 minutes, we aim for at least 100 picks to equal 300 per hour, and Amazon is satisfied with around 300–340 items per hour.

P: You count the seconds to your next break, or lunch (Yeah!), or when it is quitting time. Or this makes any Amazonian cringe. You stare at the "game" monitor. This screen shows your picking performance compared to all the other pickers working that shift. They love it when we compete against each other. What do we win? Nothing.

M: Some shifts must be easier than others. I imagine some days you may not get large heavier items at all. Do you think they give people certain stations based on the weights of the items?

P: Especially when you must bend down a lot. Some stations on certain days get mostly small light items all shift long. I refer to those nights as Walgreen nights and heavy nights as Home Depot nights. Specific picker shifts are more difficult because they require moving and replacing other items to get to heavier items. It is time-consuming and wastes energy.

M: It is like deadheading [driving with no passengers]. I am not making anything when I deadhead drive.

P: The big manager secret at Amazon is why some stations get more manageable loads, and others don't. I've asked at least twenty managers that question and have gotten six different answers, and at least ten of those managers didn't know what I meant. Do you think they are scamming us?

M: Some managers pretend not to know things. You might summarize the skills of an inexperienced manager as claiming ignorance as a response to employee questions that offends or disturbs them, especially the questions where they do not have a good answer. We call that a learned disability.

P: Anyway, I am almost home. I am exhausted. When a week of picking has ended, my first night off is a long hot bath, followed by a light dinner, and then I fall asleep trying to watch a movie that I never get through. It is a hell of a way to live your life. I don't plan to do this much longer.

M: How long have you worked for Amazonian?

P: Two years next week. I am going to try for one more year, then ask for parole. Ha Ha. Thanks for the ride home.

****

Descriptions of folks jumping to better-paying jobs, for example, going to work at Amazon, were illuminating. These are primarily people working to make ends meet during the pandemic. I found that people going to and from work tended not to share memorable stories during these rides. However, when they did share something, it was likely to be about the struggles of their work itself. Usually, they would use the Lyft ride to vent or complain. That is where their mindsets were. It was sad.

Taking people to/from work is probably not the most exciting or lucrative way to make money for Lyft, but I am genuinely interested in hearing these passenger stories. I listened to their grievances and gripes about work from the point of view of a management consultant. Now, I was trying to learn about the changes they quietly endured during the pandemic.

I heard some disturbing things like we were back in the world of assembly-line manufacturing in 1910 instead of 2022. Work performance in today's automated world of service distribution was being measured by crude and archaic means. The disturbing description of the [picker] job could be a case study of how the assembly-line world of Frederick Taylor has been resurrected. I wondered how many folks worked in such circumstances.

I wanted to tell the passenger that Taylor's Takt time was a historical anachronism, a cruelly effective measurement tool that created many troubling effects in early industrial labor practice. These kinds of techniques were brutal and Darwinian in their application. I was shocked by their resurrection in the world of service distribution work.

I felt overwhelming empathy for these exploited souls. I imagined these manual laborers spending their days in windowless warehouses around other airports, seaports, and train yards, toiling within these highly surveilled workplaces they ironically call "fulfillment centers. These workers are as invisible as the inmates in prison. If one falls out, another desperate soul takes over their workstation in seconds.

The first time I saw these vast buildings, I was amazed at their size, security, and blankness. They were about the length of six football fields. They were concrete rectangles about four-five stories high with cameras everywhere. They resembled medieval walled fortresses. An all-too-common tale emerged that the pandemic had reshaped our brave new world of the workplace into a panopticon.

Story Thirteen

Air Travel

October 9, 2021

On the next ride, I picked an atypical family on a cross-country visit that includes a scary and unexpected [and perilous] adventure. I am amazed by how we can travel these days. Stop and think of it. Some of us can physically transport ourselves to the other side of the Earth in less than 24 hours! Wealthy eople take this for granted. I do not. I am so grateful that we have the capability to drive across an entire state to visit friends and family.

P: We had a mix-up with the drive to the airport and got there late. We were the last ones to board the flight. Everyone gave us dirty looks. It was a hurried plane ride on the "low-cost carrier," as the airline calls itself. We were arguing with the flight attendant about wearing masks the entire flight. I was frustrated. All scrunched up in a plane with many tired, angry, frustrated air travelers.

M: That sounds horrendous.

P: We are a family of musicians. We were performing at a close friend's wedding in Dallas, TX. We flew to Texas, and my brother set us up at an inexpensive hotel. It was OK for the first night there because we got in late, and it was clean and quiet. But I am not sure they approved of our rugged appearance.

M: You do kind of look a little like the Addams Family? I mean that as a compliment.

P: Yeah, funny. We spent all our time practicing and playing at home this year. It was crazy playing all this new music during the last 12 months. We were dying to play in front of a live audience;

besides, we are better musicians. We're a much better band now.

M: I don't get what is so wild about your appearance? Musicians always seem theatrical to me. It is part of their charm.

P: Yeah, it is good fun. We do dress a bit extravagantly, wouldn't you say? That is part of the theater. I am Steven Tyler from Aerosmith when I perform, and my daughter has her tattoos and a few piercings. She looks like Brody Dalle. Ever heard of her?

M: No, but I bet she is great. I picked up a guy a few weeks ago who had more tattoos than that. OK, but hey, you are musicians…artists expressing yourselves. Looking to be originals, and different.

P: Yeah. In parts of Texas, some people think other means we are freaks to be locked up. The hotel people thought we were freaks and didn't exactly treat us as welcome guests. It is 2022, but it feels like 1970!

M: Well, I think of all the beautiful freaks from the Detroit music scene of the 70s and 80s? Without the freaks, life would be boring as a Texas prairie landscape!

P: Hey, I like the way you think. Lyft drivers are friendlier than that other company? They must pay you guys more, huh?

M: No, I don't think so? They leave us alone to drive where and when we please. We get messages from bots encouraging us to drive more.

P: I must tell you what we experienced last night. It was so terrifying and hilarious all at once.

M: Sure, go ahead. Our ride will take another least twenty-five minutes. I see your daughter is sleeping.

P: I told you we stayed at this Airbnb the first night in Dallas, right we could tell the hosts didn't like us being there much. They didn't even check up on us or offer us food or water. We decided for the next night [Saturday] to find a hotel. There weren't any available because the Dallas Cowboys were home that weekend.

P: My brother's place was too small for all of us, so he told us we could stay in his RV for the last night after the wedding performance.

M: OK, what kind of RV was it?

P: It was small, a class B or C kind of like a big delivery van, but it had two bunks, and both of us and the kids would be OK. My brother told us we had to put the dogs with us because they would bark all night if we slept in there without them. They won't rest in the house while you are here. Don't worry. They will lay on the floor.

P: Wow, are you sure we will all fit? Sure. It will be cozy. The wedding was a great success, and people danced and drank until about two am. My brother took care of our equipment and told us to return to the house. He said the RV was all set, and the dogs were already sleeping.

P: I will take them for a short walk and let them do their business, and then you are all set. We arrived at about two-thirty am. It started to rain.

P: I took the dogs out, and they were all excited to see us, then everyone crashed quickly, and the rain was pounding the van's roof, but we were all drained and drunk. The van started shuttering a little rocking us to sleep. Then the wind picked up and howled like steady drumming.

P: Then we were all woken up by a loud cracking noise and a whirring sound that seemed to be inside and outside the van, too. The crash made me bolt up. For a second, I didn't know where I was. My husband yelled, and the dogs began to bark. Suddenly it was terrifying.

P: The van/RV began to shake violently. Everyone was too afraid to look outside, but I did anyway. All I could see was rain coming down sideways, and the sky turned this greenish-grey, and the wind was so noisy, blowing things across the yard into the street.

P: Then, lightning struck across the street and immediately crackled that my hair stood up from the static electricity. My daughter cried out and then laughed suddenly at my hair. Then everything outside went silent. Even the dogs were scared by the silence. One was whimpering while the other tried hiding his head under the table. Then we heard debris blowing past us in the front yard like some big truck was driving back and forth.

P: This crazy whirring and crashing lasted for about thirty minutes. We were so frightened and nearly paralyzed with fear. Everyone was holding on to someone.

P: You couldn't hear because the roar of a TORNADO was blasting right next to us! My husband said later that he thought we were all going to die. "I don't want to die in this F#@&ing RV." He yelled out.

P: My daughter laughed out loud. She heard her dad swearing [he never swore in front of us EVER], and then we all abruptly stopped. My wife looked at me and just froze. Then we both started crying and hugged each other.

P: My wife freaked out about the cramped space and went to open the RV door. She stuck her head outside just a bit. The wind blew her hair extensions entirely off, and when she popped her head back in, she looked like Alice Cooper attacked by a hair dryer! We tried not to laugh, but it didn't work!

P: We all busted out laughing and screaming. I laughed so hard that I was crying. What should we do now?

P: The RV door flew open, and the camper began to jump up and down, and I thought it was about to come apart. We must get out of here. Then the dogs started barking, and I started yelling for them to stop, but my voice melted in with the thundering of the wind. Then something banged on the door. We first thought it was the house's roof or a tree smashing into the camper. It was my brother, the wind beating him back. I could hear him screaming for us to stay put.

P: Then, just like that, it all stopped. We all looked at each other in shock. Even the dogs seemed unsure about what was happening. My daughter began to soothe the dogs while I looked around the RV and asked if anyone was hurt.

P: Then my brother bangs on the door again. Zip, Is everyone all right? He said it was a tornado, all right. It blew right through the neighborhood. Hey, if no one needs help, I'm going over to Hart's house across the street. It looks like a giant tree fell on their roof!

****

The idea of flight travel during the pandemic was frightening. I imagined the likelihood of contracting the Covid-19 virus from the confines of a commercial airplane. That seemed a more significant risk than a plane crash. Everyone flying is confined in the "tube," as the airline flight crew refers. We also must not forget that the weather can produce perilous circumstances for air travel and catch us unprepared.

Spending a terrifying night in an RV and surviving a tornado is not the story I anticipated hearing from these Lyft passengers. The Dad thought it would be likelier that the plane would crash rather than them having to ride out a tornado in a camper.

This family faced the imminent peril well. They were a quirky-looking bunch, yet they were so good-natured and resilient that they found a way to laugh at what had occurred. It was like they just took the chaos in stride.

When they emerged from the RV, they found several homes nearby damaged, two wholly leveled. They immediately ran over to help the others. They removed debris and saw everyone was uninjured.

The daughter said her dad wants to buy an RV now because he thinks the vehicle was responsible for saving our family's lives. I told him he should have been a rescue worker or an EMT because he showed excellent leadership skills and an even temperament.

What impressed me about this entire family is how they had all the elements of a strong team. They had a cohesion that seemed born of hard work, respect, and collaboration. They also had some of the grit I saw in that wounded soldier. They kept each other safe and positive.

A few of them complained about their situation, yet they did something about it. The family took good care of each other while the storm wreaked havoc. They didn't let the crisis overwhelm them. And above all, they never panicked and kept their sense of humor. Their story gave the entire neighborhood [and me] an actual Lyft-no pun intended!

Story Fourteen

Battle Fatigue

October 10, 2021

Watching the road and traffic will tire you. Becoming tired will affect your ability to drive safely. Driving safely is what this is all about—a warning from an experienced truck driver.

During my Lyft driving odyssey, I didn't know how to cope with the extreme fatigue that resulted from driving several days in a row. It was unusual fatigue I had never experienced, yet it reminded me of another period in my working life where I felt similar effects. My next passenger tried to convince me that driving for long periods daily for weeks is deadly for many more reasons than I realized. He gave me some good advice for surviving on the road.

There was James, the long-haul trucker. We talked for about thirty minutes discussing the perils and challenges of driving. His advice helped me create this Guide to Exceptional Lyft Driving. Thank you, James. I drove him from his home to the truck yard, where he picked up his vehicle for the beginning of a long week of driving from Michigan to Alabama and Louisiana.

My first awareness is the number of hours I drive. If you want to earn good money, you must spend a lot of time driving. During weekdays I drive 6 hours and on weekends maybe 8 or more. However, there is a cost. It is not an easy thing to balance driving and resting. I earn between $150 to $250 a day during the regular M-F weekdays, which is about $800 to $1,000 a week in net earnings. If the weekends are busy, I can earn another $500 when I drive Saturday and Sunday. When you factor in gas, car repairs and maintenance, and health costs, I earn about $1600 a month. Not exactly much beyond subsistance level. It would be nearly impossible to live off Lyft driving alone.

My 2022 Guide to Exceptional Lyft Driving

Lyft Driving for extended periods can be an exhausting experience physically and mentally. Here are some valuable suggestions to help drivers preserve their long-term well-being.

1. Wellness Behind the Wheel begins with understanding how to prepare for a good day of Lyft driving.

    A. Be well rested before you drive.
    B. Use lumbar supports and additional seat comforts
    C. Carry enough bottled water (not sugar drinks)
    D. Carry first aid and car cleaning supplies
    E. Consider wearing a shoulder/back brace or posture harness

2. Choosing Areas to Lyft Drive and Accepting Rides

    A. Suspend judgments about picking up passengers
    B. Become aware of roads conditions in your area (potholes)
    C. Be aware of Lyft Bonus Zones
    D. Be willing to accept ANY ride requests (unless unsafe)

Long drives can be challenging, taking you away from familiar territory. It would help if you learned about ride filtering to a destination, the last ride option, and deadheading consequences to your earnings. Each of these can affect your profits and physical and mental well-being. Practicing wellness as a Lyft driver will translate to caring for passengers' well-being.

3. The Challenges of Driving Fatigue

    A. As you drive, your awareness and alertness diminish
    B. Be aware of distractions (including the Lyft app)
    C. Take regular stops to:

- Visit public restroom for body maintenance and washing hands
- Visit public places to decompress from driving concentration
- Re-adjust your seat/clean the passenger seat, door, and floor
- Make phone calls home and read your messages

D. Driving fatigue is a little like Zoom fatigue. Sitting and concentrating on a video screen causes your body to become tired and stiff from non-activity. In contrast, your brain becomes tired from processing a high degree of visual information.

E. Don't be afraid to make stops between rides!

F. Many drivers fall into the trap of driving to their destination faster, but breaking the driving day into bite-sized chunks with breaks for walks on longer journeys can help make driving feel more manageable. Taking regular breaks helps Lyft drivers to create new earning goals for their daily journeys and think of small rewards for themselves and their passengers.

4. Planning Your Meals and Staying Hydrated

By planning your meals and mealtimes while driving in advance, you can ensure that you're fully functioning both physically and mentally each day. Maintaining regular mealtimes can significantly affect a driver's well-being on the road. Don't drive on an empty stomach. Make sure you drink water regularly, even stopping at restrooms. Specific chemical imbalances can cause anyone behind the wheel to feel more damaging than if they were to have eaten.

5. Regulating Your Body (and Cabin) Temperatures

One of the biggest perks of modern cars comes from air conditioning systems. Some drivers set their car temperature and then refrain from changing it over time.

However, the temperature outside can change significantly during long driving over several hours. Maintaining a comfortable temperature in your car can also help alleviate drowsiness or distraction from extreme temperatures. Be sure to act accordingly when your body's telling you it's too cold or hot.

Driving with your windows down in cold weather can annoy passengers, so be aware of the cabin temperature and wind. Ensure your riders are comfortable.

6. Listening to Your Favorite Music Between Rides (not during rides)

We all have a list of our favorite songs in our heads. Creating an enjoyable playlist is a fun way of safeguarding a journey from feeling dull and lonely.

More voices in the car can either be a noisy distraction or help liven things up, and it's likely to take the time to fly faster on the road.

However, another idea is to create a random playlist of music you haven't heard before to keep you alert. Whether it's an album you've never got around to listening to on Spotify's Discover Weekly playlist, new music can help you stay focused – you may even uncover some new musical gems.

Alternatively, listening to podcasts can be a very engaging way of passing the time from A to B, while audiobooks may help you practice mindfulness while on the road. However, avoiding distraction from your audio is best, as this could leave you feeling unfocused and lead to potential accidents.

The future of motoring looks set to be exciting. The Lyft driving world is becoming increasingly aware of the importance of wellness and mindfulness.

However, it's encouraging to know that whether your car is your pride and joy or simply a tool to get you to where you need to be, there's always something you can do to practice wellness while at the wheel.

7. Engagement is a Passenger Reward

>   A. Gauge your passenger as they enter your car
>   B. Be polite and welcome/greet them by name
>   C. Tell them something pleasant as a welcome
>   D. Ask them their destination

If none of these pleasantries fail to engage a passenger, and they attend to their phones or appear to want to remain unengaged with you as the Lyft driver, then drive on in silence as necessary. Some people will be on the phone or otherwise engaged with something else. Only if safety becomes an issue should you compel passengers to converse. Making your Lyft rides memorable for passengers is easier than you might think. As a Lyft driver, you provide a service to passengers, and your conversations with them should be appropriate and pleasant. You may be inclined to try and optimize your earnings with tips, yet you can also begin to find ways to make their ride exceptional.

8. Exceptional rides for passengers more often come from meaningful conversations:

>   A. Meaningful conversations minus personal information share
>   B. Think of a small gift of information you might share
>   C. Small gifts may be a good restaurant or event occurring soon
>   D. Small gifts may be a book or movie of passenger interest
>   E. Small gifts may be a networking opportunity or activity

James enjoyed his trucker lifestyle three years into it. He liked the money but complained there was little time to spend it. He endured the recurring fatigue by sleeping extra hours. He said his most significant stress came from trying to make sure time deadlines. Traffic jams in big cities and construction zones thwarted the achievement of goals. He was always hungry and did not like the food on the road.

Things can be pleasant if you like to eat, and the road options are OK with your tastes. They aren't the healthiest choices. You must be careful about not eating much fast food. You will gain weight quickly, leading to other health problems.

Driving for many takes its toll. I advise Lyft drivers to find numerous ways to stay fit and alert. Getting a proper balance of rest and exercise is also incredibly important. There is no easy solution to overcoming such profound fatigue. But there are several things I have done to minimize the more disarming effects of driving [sitting] and to be able to concentrate on traffic and navigation.

When I first began Lyft driving, I knew that driving anything over one hour in my Volkswagen Jetta was potentially disabling. I am six-four inches tall. The cars today are designed for people from five-six to maybe six-foot tall. I am an outlier.

Your Lyft driver earnings will depend on how many hours you dedicate to driving and gaining knowledge of busy areas at specific times. Learning to exploit all the Lyft incentives, such as Streaks, Bonuses, and Challenges, takes a while. And please do not be afraid to take one day off, as James would say, to refresh your body and brain lest your spine and mind turn to oatmeal! James was a big friendly guy. "It's a very lonely life driving a big truck." It is just you, this big hauling machine, and the endless road. He said he would see all these beautiful places along that road but never experience them. "You merely wave as you go by and dream."

Story Fifteen

Work is Social Indeed

October 11, 2021

Work gives you meaning and purpose, and life is empty without it.
                                                    -Stephen Hawking

I pulled up to her house on the northwest side of Ypsilanti and rechecked the address. Correct, this is it. The house was in tatters. Only two cinder blocks and a short wooden plank formed the front porch. All the windows either had plastic sheeting or plywood covering their openings.

It was challenging to imagine living there. I kept looking for a "This Property is Condemned" sign. Then a young, slightly overweight woman emerged from the door carrying a torn backpack. She had fastened the backpack straps with some large safety pins and made it look like a fashionable accessory. She looked like a character in a John Steinbeck novel. Yet, as soon as Kara got into the car, I could tell the ride would be memorable. She was so excited. I said, "Hello, Kara," and she started talking. There was no need to prompt anything. She was energetic and seemed naturally curious about what it was like to Lyft drive.

P: Hi Matt. My first Lyft ride! How do you like Lyft driving?

M: Hi Kara, it is fun when I have engaging passengers like yourself. I enjoy giving rides to EMU and UM college students that don't own vehicles. Where to?

P: Student Center at EMU. I am studying for a sociology exam. I didn't have time to wait for the bus. I am very nervous about the test.

M: OK. Take a deep breath. I am a retired management professor. I know how it is with taking tests.

P: I am a junior at EMU. I just turned twenty-two yesterday, and I live alone now. My mom got sick and passed away just a few months ago. [Kara crying] she had diabetes, and heart trouble, then got the Covid-19 virus. She was sick for three weeks, and I watched her wither and die at the hospital, but I couldn't touch or hug her. I was so awful.

M: She began crying more. I pulled over. I'm so very sorry to hear that.

P: No, I apologize for crying. I can't help it. Now, I am entirely on my own. I want to finish college and be a social worker like her. I don't know how I am going to do it without her. My mom was my heart and soul. She believed in me.

M: That is wonderful. I hope you are getting some help at the University toward achieving that goal during all this. I hope you have someone to talk to and help you.

P: Yeah, they are coming to fix my house this week. It needs work, but the people at my church will work on it. They would restore it for free. My mom willed the house to me, but it needed expensive repairs.

P: The city condemned the house because the structure didn't meet the building codes. They are giving me a few weeks to fix things based on my circumstances. Once I graduate from college, I want to help people who lost their homes during the pandemic. I want to give them hope.

M: That is wonderful, Kara. You have a very noble and necessary purpose. The world needs more people like you. Just keep sharing your dreams with people who will help and guide you.

P: I want to help people, you know, do something social. I hated working alone this last year. I sat at my computer all day. Half the fun of working and learning is with other people. Don't you think?

M: I could not have said it better, Kara. You are a fantastic person, Kara. I could see that you needed help immediately when I picked you up. I am a retired professor. I was unemployed during the early pandemic, and things have been quite a struggle. I have a daughter at Adrian College. You two would make great friends.

P: Really? she said. I don't have that many friends.

M: Sure, I could give her your email address, and you could connect. Who knows, you may even become friends. We need to find a way for you to get discounted [or free] Lyft rides.

P: Wow, for real? That would be great. I don't have much money.

M: Save it for new things for your house.

P: Yeah, OK. The people from my church are coming over this Saturday. I will tell them about you.

M: You do that. I can't do more right now. I just started Lyft driving ten days ago to pay my bills.

P: Yeah, my mom was sixty-two when she got sick and died of Covid last winter.

M: I am so sorry for your loss, Kara, was it? Remember what I said about asking people for a ride. I mean it. Tell them your story, and they will share a small gift.

P: Thx, Professor Matt, for the ride. I will contact you soon. Good luck with your research, Goodbye.

****

It has been fifteen straight days of Lyft driving. This marks the halfway point of my month-long odyssey. I am starting to feel more comfortable and physically exhausted in this work. I don't plan to continue driving as much beyond the thirty days.

I meet hundreds of fascinating people Lyft driving. Many of my passengers have been absolute gems. That small minority was empathetic and giving. Most people are generous and open, but that is not always the case. We can be reshaped at any moment, subject to all sorts of internal and external influences, and change our thinking posture and behavior from moment to moment.

Some days I go back and forth ferrying students attending Eastern Michigan University (EMU) and the University of Michigan (UM). They are just five miles apart down Washtenaw Avenue. In general, one can presume that young people go to UM to become doctors, lawyers, or engineers and attend EMU to become teachers, counselors, or social workers. That assertion is a slightly oversimplified description.

Yet, it might not be surprising that I concluded having delivered about 100 student rides [of 350 during the 30-days]. I saw a pattern in this small sample emerging in these passenger types. Kara was an individual outlier and an inspirational pattern-breaker. What a generous spirit she was. She lifted me.

Lyft would probably frown on one of its drivers offering a passenger a free ride. However, this offer was off the books and had little to do with our rideshare business. Some of my passengers deserved an additional break, and a free ride was all I had to offer them beyond some study recommendations and literary resources. Remember that these stories are about exchanging small gifts. I challenge Lyft drivers in general, asking them what they share of value to their ride passengers beyond a safe and timely ride?

I can imagine all sorts of powerful ways to not only attract more Lyft passengers beyond ride discounts and conventional incentives. What if Lyft calculated ride costs based on passengers' ability to pay in addition to their current pricing equations? What if passengers could assign their tips to other needy passengers and their drivers? What if? I am sure with all the brain power working at Lyft, all these ideas are being worked out.

Story Sixteen

A Tale of Two Cities

October 12, 2021

"It was the best of times, it was the worst of times, it was the age of wisdom, it was the age of foolishness, it was the epoch of belief, it was the epoch of incredulity, it was the season of Light, it was the season of Darkness, it was the spring of hope, it was the winter of despair, we had everything before us, we had nothing before us, we were all going direct to Heaven, we were all going direct the other way – in short, the period was so far like the present period, that some of its noisiest authorities insisted on being received, for good or for evil, in the superlative degree of comparison only."

- Charles Dickens from a Tale of Two Cities

Dickens points out that the conditions he describes are like the "present period," his mid-19th century times universalizing his themes. We read these words today in the 21st century and marvel at their ringing so true even today. Above is perhaps one of the most famous first paragraphs in the literature about two cities, Paris and London. You might as well pick any two adjacent cities in America to universalize Dicken's themes. I have chosen two small university towns in Midwest America: Ann Arbor and Ypsilanti, Michigan. It is my sixteenth day of Lyft driving. It represents another of many fortunate accidents.

I present the stories in this book in the order they occurred from September 27, 2021, to October 27, 2021. This story describes the physical area [Lyft driving context] for the entire Lyft Book Project. This story occurred on the sixteenth day of Lyft driving – October 12, 2021, and resets the stage for the remaining sequence of Lyft passenger tales.

P: Eastern Michigan University [EMU] is quite different from the University of Michigan (UM). UM is a world-class research and teaching institution and collegiate athletics leader. EMU is one of the four "normal" schools designed to train teachers for the State of Michigan schools during the mid-19th century. Yet they have had a few big scandals to deal with lately.

M: If you study the history of the higher education as I have, you will find that many Ivy League graduates came to the Midwestern universities to try and replicate their eight small east coast institutions with prestigious reputations such as Harvard, Yale, Brown, Cornell, Dartmouth, Columbia, Princeton, and the University of Pennsylvania, etc.

P: Another great story about this area is the Underground Railroad that guided enslaved people north to greater freedom. The underground railroad supplied many routes to freedom, and one cut right through the Ypsilanti area due to the north-south rail lines from Toledo, Ohio. There is a statue of Harriet Tubman in Ypsilanti. I believe it is near the campus of Eastern Michigan University.

M: I know about a fascinating man named Faz Husain, elected to the Ypsilanti city council in 1979. He was the first Muslim and native of India ever to win elected office in Michigan. He campaigned for Ypsilanti to become the first city in Michigan to pass a living wage ordinance. In the early 1970s, along with neighboring city Ann Arbor, the citizens of Ypsilanti reduced the penalty for the use and sale of marijuana to a $5 civil fine. It was called the Ypsilanti Marijuana Initiative, I believe.

P: Yes, Ann Arbor has a rich history of activism, especially considering the University of Michigan's role in civil rights, political activism, free speech, and even anarchy. Many people don't know this but housed in the Hatcher Library is the most extensive collection of works on the subject of anarchy worldwide.

M: Speaking of anarchy, I understand a pop music icon named Iggy Pop is from Ypsilanti?

P: Yes, I don't know much about him, but he is called the Godfather of Punk Rock. I think he grew up in a trailer park in Ypsilanti.

M: Why are there so many trailer parks here in this area?

P: A lot of young people came to live in the area. The first significant meetings of the national left-wing campus group Students for a Democratic Society took place in Ann Arbor in 1960; in 1965, the city was home to the first U.S. teach-in against the Vietnam War. These influences washed into municipal politics during the early and mid-1970s when three members of the Human Rights Party (HRP) won city council seats on the strength of the student vote. That's a long story. Political activism is important to those living and working in the Ann Arbor area. During the 1960s and 1970s, the city became an important center for liberal politics. Ann Arbor became a locus for left-wing activism, the anti-Vietnam War movement, and the student protest movement of the 1970s.

P: In the past several decades, Ann Arbor has grappled with the effects of sharply rising land values, gentrification, and urban sprawl stretching into the outlying countryside. In 2003, voters approved a greenbelt plan under which the city government bought development rights on agricultural parcels of land adjacent to Ann Arbor to preserve them from sprawling development. Since then, the local debate has focused on how to accommodate and guide development within city limits. Still, I believe Ann Arbor is one of the best cities in the United States. Especially for an old, retired teacher like me.

Here is my stop. Thx. UM Rackham Graduate School.

M: Enjoy the lecture.

****

I began each Lyft driving day with a simple goal to engage my passengers and ask if they were willing to share a good story. I also started each new day by driving to a slightly different starting place or at another time of day. I was looking to gain variety, offsetting the habit of driving in the same locale and avoiding the patterning of passenger ride requests. I would often navigate a line equally between Ypsilanti and Ann Arbor and see where my driving fortunes turn.

It was my daughter's idea that I drive for Lyft. She encouraged me to practice job crafting and make the job of moving people around town more enjoyable. You will see what I mean as we proceed. It was my wife's urging me to research as I did as a professor and Esther encouraging me to write a book that continues to astound me.

As a Lyft driver, I am interested in people's stories and the traveling patterns that emerge from what I do. I am amazed at the variety I encounter each day. Everyone has their own unique story to tell. I marveled at how every story was so amazing. Generally, people are incredibly interesting for the most part. They want someone to listen to them. As a Lyft driver, that was very important to note.

One interesting difference between Ann Arbor and Ypsilanti is the general road/street pavement conditions. In Ypsilanti, I must be more vigilant when driving nearly everywhere because there are potholes in the streets. Not to say that Ann Arbor didn't have a good share of potholes. In Ann Arbor, the main obstacles to local travel were construction zones where they were repairing the road surfaces. In Ann Arbor, construction and road repaving seemed to be on every other neighborhood block. So, I explain the driving differences by the number of unpaved obstacles we must avoid.

Story Seventeen

Circuits and Strange Loops

October 13, 2021

I picked up a young couple at the DTW airport. We talked about his being a postdoc in aerospace engineering and beginning his work for NASA. And wouldn't you know he was going to the NASA Ames Research Center, where I had been a summer volunteer back in 2008? I resisted telling my story [no easy chore], favoring him telling me about how he came to accept a position at NASA Ames Research. It was a fantastic day of mystery, strange loops, and serendipity! He knew the same people I knew and was surprised I described the Ames Research Center (ARC) so well. Here is one dandy of a story.

P: It all started with a joke. My closest friends began to joke with me about my slow progress in earning a Ph. D. They warned me about becoming a "Lifer RA," a graduate student research assistant that never actually graduates. One who never completes their doctoral degree by completing the dissertation, sadly labeled for life, ABD… All But Dissertation.

M: I nearly succumbed to the very same sad designation as well. It is every doctoral student's fear.

P: It began as just good fun. My department colleagues started this funny competition, sending me outrageous job postings by email to amuse themselves. Several of them kept in touch with me after graduating and would send emails encouraging me to get serious, finish my damn degree and get a real career, not a post-doc. They all sent me strange job postings. The crazier, the better (always cc-ing them to each other). I got all sorts of wonderfully silly job postings by email, for example, several zookeepers and beekeeper positions, sherpas in Nepal to ant hill removal technicians in Botswana, soap demonstrator, whisker twister, assistants to all sorts of crazy, mixed-up people, leather polisher, rickshaw driver, food tasters in Somali and Siberian prison camps, construction workers in Mongolia, animal trainers in a traveling circus, etc. You get the idea.

P: My best friend even sent me a few postings that matched the ones that were jokes. One was a job at NASA. The subject line read, Immediate opening sent exclusively to Rocket Boy. He started to refer to me as Rocket Boy [RB] to my other friends, and they all started calling me that, which annoyed me.

M: Sorry, that last bit was funny.

P: The job posting from NASA was for aeronautical engineering research. The more I looked at it, the more it sounded like the perfect job. That was interesting. I must have read it four or five times. I sent him a reply saying I thought I would apply. But you haven't graduated yet, you fool. was his retort. I got a strange message signed by six of my colleagues. It read:

1) Upon applying for the Rocket Boy/Fighter Jet Engineer (RBFJE) position: If and only if secures a phone interview with NASA Ames Research human resources. Then and only then will he receive one case of imported beer (his choosing) delivered to his home within ten days of the phone interview date.

2) If and only if RB secures a physical visit and interview to ANY NASA Center in relationship to this application, then RB will receive a (coupon for dinner at a top restaurant in Mountain View, CA, for himself and five guests); and

3) if RB secures an actual job offer for the RBFJE position, then the Group of AE Docs will pay for a five-day cruise from Miami, FL.,

to the Grand Bahama Island (including airfare and meals) for RB and one guest. All six had signed the document.

P: What did I have to lose? I received an email confirming the challenge. So, I signed the document indicated and returned the scan to my friend for validation. It simply said, "Please Apply Now." I sent in a concise, neat packet of application documents to NASA human resources primarily for fun. Still, I made it a serious application, and besides…who knows…maybe a dissertation idea will emerge out of it all. I mailed off the envelope and quickly forgot about the challenge, hoping my colleagues would too.

P: Two weeks later, the landline phone rang in the afternoon. I heard my partner answer the phone in the other room. "NASA…we don't know anyone from NASA," she said. I yelled out, "DON'T HANG UP. I'll get it." I rushed to take the phone. She stood there sneering while I said, "Hello, yes, this is Spencer." The voice on the other side was stern yet calm and relaxed, all business with an unmistakable military bearing.

P: A voice began, "My name is Mr. Martin at NASA Ames Research Center. Is this Spencer H. of Ann Arbor, MI? I said yes. I am turning you over to Barb Gunderson at the Planner's Collaborative. She will arrange a phone interview for the NASA Ames Research Aeronautics Engineering position. Is that acceptable to you, Mr. H. Yes. Yes, sir, it is. All I asked Barb to do was to send me an email confirming the phone interview would take place in three days. I was surprised (and ecstatic) because I had already picked out a case of Belgian beer. I planned to call My friend that evening to place my order!

M: So, let me get this straight. Your friends from graduate school played this joke on you. You went along with it. Then it turned into a genuine opportunity, and now you were going to have a real job interview with the folks at NASA. Incredible.

P: Yeah, isn't it. It gets better. I copied the NASA email and sent it off. They were all surprised and optimistic. My friend thought it would be just my luck that I get hired by NASA on a joke posed by my UM friends. I remember the phone interview lasted about twenty-five minutes, and it was very general and went like a fun conversation.

P: I also remember telling my partner I thought the NASA phone interview went surprisingly well. My friend sent me well wishes and said my case of Belgian beer was being FedEx-ed, and it should arrive in a day or two. I tried calling each UM group member to gloat about my interview. They were all very pleased I had gotten through the interview successfully and received the expensive beer. They told me it was well worth seeing me so upbeat about my future for a change.

M: I think a few of my friends were surprised by how I turned this around on them. I kept thinking that they would all back out.

P: Exactly two weeks after the phone interview, the phone rang again. This time I was there to answer. It was Mr. Martin, again sounding like a major general. He told me they were pleased with my interview and wanted to know if I would like to visit Johnson Space Center in Houston, Texas. I could hardly contain myself. I'm going to NASA!

P: I think I said, "really?" four times. I am handing you over to Barb. See you in Houston next week, Spencer." I immediately emailed, "Rocket Boy ordered to report to NASA Mission Control." Three days later, there was a check in the mail for $600 with a note signed by the group, Have a great NASA visit. Have dinner on us! I told them I felt like a ten-year-old. It kept getting better and better.

P: I arrived in Houston on a sunny Wednesday afternoon. I was given a whirlwind tour of Mission Control and escorted to a test pilot/astronaut meet-up. I was overwhelmed with child-like wonder and a slack-jaw. I spent two days listening to people talk about the Mercury, Gemini, and Apollo space programs. I also got a different take from those people on the aeronautics side of NASA. One fellow even said to me, "Listen, always remember the NASA means the National "Aeronautics" [first] and Space Administration [second].

P: I learned more about this meaning when I was shuttled over to Mountain View, CA, to visit the Ames Research Center (ARC), located at the southern end of San Francisco Bay at a base called Moffett Field. Moffett is one of the oldest airbases in the US that houses the largest functioning wind tunnel in the world capable of MACH 1 speed simulation with a Boeing 737 hanging on a stinger inside.

M: Wow, Satellites, rocket planes, and moon rockets are built and tested there. I read that pilots train in the most sophisticated flight simulator there, and astrobiologists experiment with cultivated bacteria to test their survival capability in space, and other NASA projects.

P: All true. There were a lot of [moments] during that visit that will last me a lifetime. I wrote dozens of emails to my family and friends about the experiences. The more time I spent there, the more I began to see the real possibilities of working at NASA, but I still had mixed feelings about it. All of that is another story. Barb was amazing, acting as my NASA tour guide and search committee liaison. She had worked there for almost 20 years and seemed to know everyone and everything. She was friendly and cheerful; we seemed to hit it off well. She didn't tip her hand about me or the selection process.

The only thing she said that got me excited was the moment when she dropped me off at the SF airport. I stepped out of the car, and she leaned over the passenger seat and said, "I think the committee is leaning toward you." Then she drove off.

M: OMG, I think I am going to work at NASA Ames. I remember talking to my friend and the entire group later that week about this amazing prospect.

They jokingly asked if they should be looking at cruise pamphlets. I told them they didn't need to fulfill the final reward. I told them that the entire experience so far was reward enough, but they were adamant, and all said they were in it for the entirety.

P: For the next couple of weeks, I was walking on air. I completely forgot about all the stress of my doctoral program. I wanted to tell all my colleagues about the NASA visit and the opportunity, but I resisted my partner's advice," Wait until it's real," she kept saying. My friend was as excited as I was, already planning our cycling routes in Marin County. If I were out there, we would join the various groups of cyclists that regularly ride around the Marin Headlands out to Point Reyes and around Mt. Tamalpias over to Stinson Beach, CA.

P: Because the calls came two weeks after they notified me, I was on pins and needles that day. The time I expected the call came and went. No call. I convinced myself that it meant nothing. NASA would surely call tomorrow. I felt optimistic. The group told me to hang in there. They would be lucky to have me. Stay positive and stay tuned.

P: One evening My closest friend gave me a call. After thinking it was NASA when it rang, I told him I was pleased he didn't play the obvious joke and faked the call. I said I didn't get the offer. He was upbeat, reminding me that the group thought this entire challenge was great. He didn't care about the cost. The group wanted me to keep some of the beer for a future reunion.

M: My friend said something that has always stuck with me, "You know when I saw this posting at NASA, my first impression was what I thought of you. Only after that did I think of all the joking we did at your expense, how well you took it all in stride, and how well this idea of a NASA engineer fit my personality. I am always rooting for you."

M: That's a good friend.

P: I was grateful because had it not been for him sending me the advertisement (even in jest), I would have never visited NASA Ames Research Center, etc.

P: At the three-week mark, the phone finally rang. Again, it was Mr. Martin. He began by saying the selection committee impressed me and wanted you to know when I could start. They said there was only one hitch. Your credentials and experience are just right. However, the committee is concerned that you have not completed your graduate degree. So here is their offer to you:

P: Given our mutual needs, we can hire you in a slightly different role. We need a young, innovative engineer with the latest skills and education, and you need a good job [and possibly a boost for your dissertation research], so we propose you join us as an aeronautical engineering "assistant research director" for two years, at a similar entry-level salary for engineers. Does that sound acceptable to you. When can you start?

P: Immediately, I mean as soon as I return from the cruise I booked months ago, Mr. Martin.

P: He said, Enjoy your holiday, and then we will see you at the ARC.

****

As a Lyft driver, I became sensitive to passenger behaviors. Some were relatively innocuous and simple, and others were disturbing. The disturbing patterns were more interesting to me. For example, some passengers ignored me completely once the ride began. Others babbled away or offered wholly uninteresting stories that were shallow and mundane. I had little success redirecting these passengers once they started telling such stories. They thought their stories were exceptional candidates for my book, but too many stories were forgettable and dull. I endured these passenger tales.

The most interesting were stories of descriptive experience and emotional depth. Some were evidence of magic like this one. They were like tossing stones in a pond, concentric circles. They had intriguing beginnings, puzzling middles, and endings revealing empathy and authentic connection. My best Lyft passenger stories were strange loops: connections between our useful fictions and earthly enactments.

I called these stories strange loops, compelling patterns I recognized when familiarity gave way to a new kind of order that emerged from the chaos, a fresh perspective. A typical strange loop pattern was stories told that circled me back to where I started either physically [locale] or psychologically [sense of home, the comfort of familiarity, etc.]. In other words, each day, I set off from my house into the unknown strangeness of the world around me and returned home. My daughter described Lyft driving as a minor [or daily] Homeric odyssey.

How closely connected [not separated], we all are and how what we do daily is heavily influenced by trying to keep some strange loops open and close others. I was constantly surprised by how many passenger stories correspond strongly with my experiences. It was always wonderful to learn that the world is small, meaning there may be fewer degrees of separation between you and a stranger than you can imagine. Discovering this was what I believe drives the serendipity and, more importantly, our urge to organize.

One young man got into my car today and started telling me about "another Lyft driver" that told him a wild story about how he was writing a book about Lyft driving and collecting passenger stories. At first, I was confused by what he was saying. He didn't realize that I was that Lyft driver.

Story Eighteen

Daydreams and Nightmares

October 14, 2021

(Come in under the shadow of this red rock),
And I will show you something different from either
Your shadow at morning striding behind you
Or your shadow at evening rising to meet you;
I will show you fear in a handful of dust.

- T. S. Eliot - The Waste Land

Part 1: Morning Daydreams

M: Lyft driving is fun to do for the most part. My first challenge is, "should I drive in the AM or PM?" Lyft does a great job providing information to help you decide. The dilemma involves an interesting tradeoff. Many early morning rides are shorter, usually taking people to work or shop locally. There also are a fair number of rides to the airport or hospitals. However, if you drive in the later evenings or at night, you risk having more sketchy passengers with the usual behavioral issues from fatigue or intoxication. Here is an example:

What attracted me initially to Lyft driving was that I could drive around the cities of Ypsilanti and Ann Arbor and eat anywhere I chose.

Autumn is a feast for the senses. It is my favorite time of year. We Michiganders are fortunate to have spectacular, fifty-foot sugar maple trees all over our property. When my daughter was young, she asked me why the trees changed color. I told her that as a scientist, the leaves change color as their acid levels determine; as a minister, the leaves change color to herald nature's design; and as a poet, the leaves change as a sign of beauty before death. "Which one are you, Dad?" "No clear reason you can't be all three!"

I decided to Lyft drive during the day because of the simple fact that I can see better. I thoroughly enjoy the natural scenery. I enjoyed cruising outside Ann Arbor, where many winding country roads have rows of spectacular trees changing color. I would start on these splendid fall days, and I didn't care if I got any ride requests. I would daydream while driving, imagining the progress of my book project corresponded to the brightness of the trees, and I was reveling in its completion. Would people want to read it? Who knows?

Then I soon realized something much more profound. Every time I picked up a passenger, I would have to give up one of my favorite pleasures: daydreaming. As soon as I accepted a ride, I would obligingly push a button on my phone accepting a Lyft ride request and simultaneously pushing a button in my mind: the punch-clock time-to-work button.

This morning I was dreaming of interviewing the sixteenth-century writer and philosopher Michel de Montaigne whose work I greatly admired [yes, I dream of such things]. I dreamed of also taking my retirement at 38 years old to read and write as he did. However, I missed that goal by some twenty-five odd years.

Montaigne had this fantastic way of making one feel good in their skin, especially in his later essays. He had a preoccupation with aches and pains from an unfortunate riding accident and discussed how to die well in vivid detail, having inherited this art from his Greek influencers. Yet he was a most joyous epicurean who wrote extensively about all sorts of sensual pleasures and aesthetics. Many sensual driving pleasures come from simply observing and experiencing life in the world.

Part 2: Evening Nightmares

Lyft passengers will tell you horrific stories on occasion. One typical type of story may be the Lyft driver-murder story. I am confident that every Lyft driver has one. Here is mine.

I wasn't quite a month into my Lyft adventure when this unfortunate experience occurred. I don't usually drive after it gets dark. The reasons include the general feeling that passengers are different at night. More people are doing sketchy things at night, even during the pandemic.

I took a ride request on the west side of Ann Arbor, and I thought it was a seemingly ordinary ride. I hit the last ride button. I had difficulty finding the correct address because I couldn't see the address number from the street. There were no streetlights close. Finally, I pulled into a driveway, and out of nowhere, four young people rushed into my car, and they all got in the back seat quickly.

M: Wait, wait, I can't take four riders.

P: Sure, you can. It's not fair.

They were all laughing and trying to squeeze into my VW Jetta. One of them made a couple of rude comments. I turned and said that passengers of mine don't talk like that in my car. I was too tired to argue; it was my last ride, and it looked like I would make my number for the day.

P: Where you from, dog?

M: I am from the hood, east side of Detroit, a retired professor.

P: Damn boy, you're a genuine 313, and now you're a Lyft driver.

M: They all laughed. I was starting to get angry because he was dissing me. I decided to drive and not engage with him. Once on the freeway, we darted toward Ypsilanti. There were two stops. The first one was at a rundown building where another young man came out and handed a camera and a brown paper bag to the young man sitting next to the window in the back seat. I couldn't tell what was in the paper bag, but I could see it wasn't a bottle. I thought it was batteries. He handed the two items through the window and dashed back into the building—the girl behind me.

P: Let's go, Jeeves.

P: Do you believe in God?

M: What kind of question is that? I almost stopped the car on the expressway. The young man with a sharp tongue and angry eyes stared at me.

P: Cool down, driver-man. No need to get pissed off.

M: I wanted them out of my car. They were rude, and I had no idea what they were doing. It was about a mile to the second stop. When I pulled into the parking lot of a motel, I unlocked the doors, and they all jumped out. I opened both front windows so some other people in the lot could hear us. The young woman who asked me the question hung back and stood beside my door almost as if she were guarding me.

M: The two young men, one carrying a paper bag and the other, walked to the door and began filming. The other young man pulled a handgun from the paper bag and approached the motel door. At that moment, I turned toward the driver-side window of my car, and the woman was leaning down to say something to me in a whisper.

P: Are you a cop?

M: Then she cocked her head to signal to me that I should scram. I didn't wait to answer her. I hit the gas and sped into the street without looking back. My heart was beating so hard I could feel it in my jaw. I thought my head was about to explode. I kept waiting for a bullet to hit the back of the car. I think I even let out a scream.

M: I remember telling myself that I will never Lyft drive at night again.

M: I didn't drive straight home. I went across the street to a Mcdonald's and tried to call the police. I dialed the local sheriff's office. But like in one of those NCIS shows on TV, five squad cars suddenly pulled into the parking lot where these folks were. I thought the police were about to start shooting, so I drove away quickly. My hands were shaking. I kept thinking about that young woman asking me those questions. What was she trying to do? Scare me?

****

It is difficult enough capturing this story and reliving it. I choose to archive such scary experiences. They serve no purpose other than recalling fear. When I think about that ride, I try and steer the terrible thoughts into the ether before my mind gets too far into the darker details. Sometimes a threatening passenger takes me down a rabbit hole of fear. It doesn't happen very often. I still have a hard time thinking about what might have happened compared with what occurred. Imagination stirs my memory.

My only advice to Lyft drivers: We know driving all day wreaks havoc on our physical and mental health. The constant concentration combined with sitting still for long periods is wrenching. I know my brain turns to oatmeal if you don't take walking/stretching breaks and provide myself with vigorous physical stimulation.

I do most of my driving before it gets dark. Night ride requests often take me to unfamiliar areas [sometimes incentivized by the benign Lyft bonuses] that may be more unsafe at night. It is more likely that late evening passengers will be intoxicated. On occasion, their story depicts crimes they may or may not have committed or descriptions of their experience being in jail.

To put this experience into context. I delivered 350 Lyft rides during my first thirty days, and this was the only one I felt my life was in danger. I realized when this ride experience occurred how vulnerable I am as a driver. I am not the type to carry a weapon for protection, yet I felt utterly unprotected and alone that night. It only takes one instance like this to abandon Lyft driving altogether.

The truth is that GPS is dumb in a way that is important to your safety. It can lead you to abandoned home addresses and sometimes take you into potentially dangerous neighborhoods. I decided to drive during the day simply because it is much safer.

I also resolved to pay closer attention to the Lyft customers I accepted ride requests from considering their travel destinations. I know I can always refuse to provide the rideshare service if I feel unsafe. So, don't be afraid to act in your best interest and keep your antennae up even in your neighborhood.

Story Nineteen

A Close Call

October 15, 2021

Luck is a surprise dressed in serendipity. The Universe whispers its serendipity through us all. It is difficult to hear a clearer message through all the background noise.

During a high-speed lane change, a near accident occurs because of tiredness, distraction, and impaired vision. It was a scary moment after experiencing a very dangerous spin-out. I drove around in tight local circles for about five hours when a ride request came across town.

M: I pushed the "Last Ride" button on my Lyft Driver app. It was already dark when I usually call it quits, but I wanted to make my number before I went home for the day. "Making my number" means earning at least $125-$150 daily.

M: I got on the I-94 expressway and headed east toward Detroit. As I exited the crisscross part of the exit, a car suddenly appeared on my right, attempting to pass me at high speed. I slowed down to let him pass, but he panicked and suddenly hit his breaks hard enough to make his car swerve, glancing off the corner of my front bumper [or at least that is what it felt like].

M: In a split second, I was spinning off the exit ramp veering off the shoulder, and stopping about fifty feet in the grass. I felt visibly shaken by the force of the slide. Then my car stopped.

M: I jumped out of the car, hoping I could get the license plate number. As fast as it happened, the other vehicle was gone.

M: I stood there, both hands shaking, cursing under my breath. I looked at my car, and there seemed to be no damage. There was a lot of mud and grass on my tires. I couldn't even find a mark where I thought the other person hit me. Maybe they didn't hit me? Was I the one that made a driving error? I didn't quite know.

M: I called my wife. She immediately said, "Is anything wrong?" I didn't want to scare her for no reason. I finished driving for the day and headed home.

M: As I started home, I began thinking about my mortality. I remembered this quote from a Mitch Albom book I read a few years back "Everyone knows they are eventually going to die, but no one believes it."

M: The very next day, October 20, I decided not to drive. I am not sure what it was. I felt like the incident the previous day was perhaps a warning. Anyway, that is the way I interpret things. "Perhaps something is telling you to rest?" is what my wife said. So, I told my wife that I decided to visit this young man named Paul, that started a van conversion business in NW Detroit called Drifter Vans. I had been meaning to visit the place for months and now seemed to be a good time. I pulled up to his Drifter Van shop, which was challenging to find.

M: Hello Paul. I am excited to meet you because I have been researching Class B recreation vehicles for a few years. I hope to own one someday, perhaps if my book sells. Ha Ha.

P: Hi Matt, great to meet you. Welcome to Drifter Vans! So, you are writing a book? About what?

M: Well, a couple of weeks ago, I started Lyft driving at the suggestion of my wife and daughter, and now I am collecting passenger stories. I am a semi-retired professor.

M: Listen, I know this isn't a Lyft ride, but I wonder if I might interview you and get your story? I am fascinated by your business, and I want to learn more. Fifteen-twenty minutes tops, about the length of my average Lyft ride! Do you have some time for a few questions?

P: Sure, fire away.

M: How did you get started doing this?

P: Well, Matt, do you want the short or extended versions? Ok, short. It all started with a backpacking trip to South America. I was previously addicted to opiates and was a couple of years sober. Although I was reclaiming my life, I was still missing something. This trip was supposed to be one month and turned into a 1-year journey that changed my life forever. What I realized I was missing was a passion.

P: I realized that adventure travel enriched my life, and I made it my life purpose to travel and help others experience the same thing that enriched my life. I had been working in construction for 20 years, so building campervans made sense! I could be in an industry around other passionate travelers and build a tool for people to travel in!

M: You are a man after my own heart. Are people buying more small RVs these days? I mean, the Class B camper vans or, as you call them, transit conversion vans?

P: The transit or sprinter vans [like you see Amazon drivers drive] are a trendy platform these days. It is expensive to haul a Class A 40-footer around. I guess part of it was from that movie, Nomadland. Many people live in these small RVs today. The pandemic made my business explode. I have only been doing this for a few years. I used to own a food truck, and that was when I got the idea to build RVs out of transit vans. My real passion is travel. This business combines my passion with my construction experience!

M: Wow, this is great. I can see how each step in the conversion process works. How much do they cost?

P: Well, the initial transit van can cost between $55 - $80 thousand, and the conversion averages another $50-$60K. It depends on your desired level of luxury.

Paul and I stepped outside. He had been very generous with me, and I didn't want to take any more of his time. I wasn't thinking of how Paul's story might fit into the book. Besides, he hadn't been a Lyft passenger. Yet that was about to change.

M: Hey Paul, thanks a lot. I think I have enough to write a good story. That is one cool Jeep parked there. Grand Wagoneer?

P: Yeah, we just got done detailing and cleaning it up. It is my uncle's new Jeep.

M: By the way, I didn't ask you. Do you have any family here in Detroit?

P: Yes, I do. I live with my uncle right now, and I have a fiancé, but she is back in Bolivia. She will be here for a visit soon. Come by again in a few weeks and meet her.

M: That is very gracious of you, Paul. I promise to send you a copy of the chapter story I will write from this visit and conversation [we shook hands]. Thank you very much. What does your uncle do?

P: Oh, he is a writer. He is very well-known here in Detroit. You probably heard of him. His name is Mitch Albom.

M: What did you say? Mitch Albom is your uncle? Mitch Albom, Tuesday's with Morrie Mitch Albom?

P: Yeah, no kidding. I live with him.

M: Mitch Albom, the author, is your uncle! I cannot believe this. Do you remember what I told you about what happened yesterday? I thought of the quote from Tuesdays with Morrie after I spun out of the exit ramp.

P: Wow, I guess the Universe is listening to you, Professor!

****

I had a tough time sleeping the previous night after the close call. Driving was exhausting me. It was not the sore back and neck that affected me as much as my shortened attention span and mental fatigue. I knew I needed a much deeper rest.

The only dangerous moment I experienced as a Lyft driver taught me about aging, fatigue, distractions, and vigilance. There may have been a dramatic accident had I not been able to adjust quickly. Yet I still believe I initially made a poor decision to accept the nightmare ride.

Being more unaware of driving dangers felt like riding a bike in heavy traffic. The combined effects of weather, fatigue, darkness, distraction, noise, multi-tasking, and not listening to your own body can produce dangerous situations. Lyft driving helped me become more aware of avoiding hazardous conditions and potential accidents. Yet despite the dangers were those fortunate accidents I wanted to capture.

I am not very good at multi-tasking. When you drive for Lyft, you must pay attention to the traffic while frequently glancing at the Lyft app on your phone. I had found that mounting my phone to the dashboard made it easier to glance at while driving at high speed. I have an older iPhone 7, a relatively small device with a small visual screen. I am constantly straining to read what is on my tiny screen. I cannot afford the latest versions of anything, so I tend to use older technology until forced to upgrade. No wonder younger people today don't buy cars. They must spend nearly as much on a phone as I did on a car when I was their age. My first car cost me $1450 back in 1972.

Had I not experienced such a dangerous moment the previous day, which I took as a warning, I would not have taken the day to rest. I would have missed an opportunity. I listen more closely now to the messages of my conscience. It is my advice to those doing this kind of work.

Serendipity comes from out of nowhere if we are open to it. I believe it does all the time, and we often miss it. I could not have imagined a better time to meet Paul than when I met him. Even though he wasn't a Lyft passenger in the strictest sense during this odyssey, his recent acquaintance taught me some important lessons. I am hoping we become better friends.

Story Twenty

Always Go Home

October 17, 2021

The concept of home equals safety and security to most of us; and for me the promise of rest.

This Going Home story illustrates the pleasure [security] of visiting your past. Each day of Lyft driving, I start with the renewed spirit of adventure driving me. And EVERY Lyft ride should be like going home. I never know what I am going to experience day to day. During these 30-days, I tended to love the days when someone shared a story with me that made me think of my past or the positive future. This story traces one passenger returning to where he (we] grew up, surprisingly not far from my neighborhood. It was such a magical story that ended a great day of my Lyft driving adventure.

M: The platform sends me the usual messages from Lyft. It is asking me if I would provide a ride to this customer again in the future? That signals that I am ready to accept the next ride; this time, it immediately said I had already arrived. I was confused. The passenger's name was Dan. The app said he was right there. "There" meant the DTW domestic arrivals drop-off area, but I couldn't figure out whom Dan was among the many people staring at their phones.

M: I looked across the street toward the airport parking structure. Then, a man stopped and yelled at me, "Hey, are you my Lyft driver by chance?" and I said Yes! So, I waved him over and picked him up. Wow, I didn't even have to move to pick up my next rider. I picked Dan up at the DTW airport around six pm.

M: Where are we headed, Dan?

P: Harper Woods. Do you know it?

M: Oh, yes. I grew up close to there over by Eastland Mall.

M: From where were you flying?

P: Atlanta. I am back in town for my 50th high school reunion. I went to South Lake High in St. Clair Shores.

M: Wow, I went to East Detroit HS just down the street from South Lake HS on 9 Mile Road! We were rival schools! What year did you graduate? 1971? I graduated in 1974. How cool.

P: Yeah, it is exciting. I am visiting my parent's home, where my sister now lives with my 87-year-old mom. My dad passed away a few years back. I cannot wait to see my old swimming teammates; four will be there, and I haven't seen them since high school!

M: You were on South Lake HS's swim team?

P: Yes, sir, I was the co-captain of the South Lake High School swim team in 1971.

M: OMG! I was on East Detroit High School's swim team when we won the state championship. We must have competed with your team that year. I was only a sophomore. I just barely made the team, but I remember swimming in that meet because my mother came to watch me swim.

P: Yeah, you guys beat us good. But I held my own in the 200 Individual Medley. I came in second. Wow, you remember, huh?

M: We had two great IM swimmers that year. Both went to Indiana to train for the Olympics. One got killed in a car accident the following year. I swam the 100-yard breaststroke. Isn't it amazing that we must have been at that same swim meet 50 years ago! A fascinating coincidence.

P: Yeah, it sure is.

M: So, what do you say to your old high school teammates you haven't seen for a half-century?

P: Yeah, I have been thinking about meeting my old school buddies. I don't remember my high school days. I want to see them and have a few laughs.

M: Yes. I can visit my mother after I drop you off. She lives about two miles from here.

P: Hey, look! There is my high school. It looks the same, but it seems smaller. Mind if we pull over so I can take a couple of pictures? The gift of this is seeing my old neighborhood.

M: Sure.

P: My mother always told me that if I ever get lost or depressed. I should always come home. I don't think I ever took her up on that offer much. Now, it seems I need to visit her to recharge her batteries.

M: That is one way to look at it.

P: Thanks for stopping. The plan is to take many photos this time. Do you mind taking one with me in the picture and the school behind me? I want to send it to my school buddies tomorrow.

M: Good idea. Maybe you can find a yearbook picture and put them side-by-side for them?

P: Hey, let me tell you a quick story about our twenty-fifth high school reunion. You'll love this. A few weeks before the reunion, a few of us that rode motorcycles decided to take a little road trip, film it, and share the videos and photos at the reunion.

We met east of St. Louis, figuring it was an equal distance for everyone and an excellent place to start our adventure. Everyone wanted to go to Memphis, TN, mostly because none of us had ever been there, and a few wanted to visit Graceland. Well, we headed down there, and man, did it rain. We had to pull up maybe six times and wait out the thunderstorms. It was still fun riding with the gang. They all had dressed out Harleys, and I had an old Indian, and everyone was envious.

Anyway, one afternoon we were about thirty minutes west of Memphis riding along when my buddy signaled that he had to pee. The only place to go was in the corn field, so we all pulled over and rushed into the field. While I was whizzing, this old hound dog lumbered right up to me and started yelping. It was funny, but it is hard to piss when you have a dog howling at you. Then I heard this old farmer [F] yelling for the dog to get along. I thought he meant us.

He walked up behind us and said you probably would have to pee in my corn if you didn't drink all that beer! We all laughed and finished up our business in the corn. The old man asked us where we were headed. He asked us if we had ever heard of Jenny's Mud. Folks didn't know, but he brewed it on his farm. It was a very popular beverage. So, we all got back on our bikes as he pointed where we should park for a sit-down visit.

We assembled in front of his barn, passed around these giant mugs, then produced what looked like a small keg where he filled each glass. It was powerfully good stuff. We had a good laugh. I turned my attention to inside the barn, where I saw a car underneath a giant tarp. I asked the old man what kind of car it was. He told us it was a 1929 Ford he got from his father. Can we see it? Sure, as he walked over to pull the tarp away. Does it run?

F: I don't know.

I looked around the barn and saw another interesting vehicle in a corner with boxes, crates, hay bales, and junk covering it up. I lifted an old blanket then I saw it. Unmistakable. It was an Indian motorcycle. I asked him whose motorcycle it was. He didn't know. It has been there ever since I can remember. I have one right outside, but this looks like a special edition.

P: Mind if I take a closer look? Be my guest said the old man. Is it for sale? Oh, no.

So, I took the blankets and other junk off the bike to see it better, perhaps identify the year it was built. There were parts of the motorcycle missing, and then I found a box that contained some of the lights, hand grips, and the seat. I pulled the seat out of the box and wiped it off. Then we all gasped at what we saw written on the back of the seat. It read, To Elvis, Love Priscilla. Can you imagine?

P: Hey Matt, this has been great. I never expected my Lyft ride would be this kind of pleasure. Thanks for bringing me to my high school. I don't think it was on the GPS, so I know you did it intentionally. You are a great Lyft driver! Oops, there is my mom's street.

M: Best of luck, Dan. It was great meeting you, and we had a wonderful visit and 50th-year reunion.

****

Aristotle wrote that there were only two kinds of movement: moving in a straight line, with the four fundamental elements demonstrated [fire, air, water, and earth] in perfect motion [circular], which is only possible by celestial bodies of the heavens. The moon, the sun, and the known planets of that time traveled in perfect circles around the earth. That cosmology explains Aristotle's argument that the heavens are perfectly harmonious with the planet earth and human beings.

For many reasons, this was one of my favorite Lyft rides. Dan was my age and a very upbeat man. He was excited to be visiting Michigan. It was effortless, like I was out driving with a friend.

The cool thing was when I asked Dan where he was going, he enthusiastically said, "To the NE side of the Detroit suburbs." Hey, that is where I grew up. The destination was a few miles from where my mother lived.

I called her after dropping Dan off at his 50th high school reunion in St. Clair Shores. We reminisced and laughed about the things were had in common. Then I visited my mother to tell her more about my recent Lyft Driving adventures [except the Close Call].

I told her I enjoyed Lyft driving primarily because I had gathered many great stories. I am not sure how much I would be enjoying it had I not job-crafted this work into a book/research project. I wasn't making much money, and my car was getting destroyed by the road potholes.

I wondered how other Lyft drivers felt the same. I had collected passenger stories. Perhaps other Lyft drivers did, but how many wrote them down? I was curious but not interested enough to spend my time trying to connect with other drivers online.

I ended the twentieth day by deadheading back home after having a lovely visit and tea with my eighty-five-year-old mother. It was a perfect ending to a very long day of Lyft driving. I began to think about what to do after I finished the book.

Story Twenty-One

Self-Driven Engineers

October 18, 2021

"I put my heart and soul into my work and have lost my mind in the process."

-Vincent Van Gogh

Two computer science [software] engineers first try and explain how autonomous vehicles work, then provide a fascinating take on automation and technology, which they believe will solve our public transportation problems. They evangelized technology's potential and the current work creating their driving Triple As: artificial intelligence, applications, and algorithms. Two young Asian men get in my car. They look like students. One was named Feng [F], and the other was Zixin [Z].

M: Hello, Feng and Zixin. Did I get that right? Where to? Off to class?

F: UM North Campus. No, we are recent UM graduates. We are recruiting at the School of Engineering and LSA Computer Science departments.

M: OK, for what types of work? Software engineering and Artificial Intelligence design mainly.

F: We work for two tech companies that you probably know.

Z: I work on a software development team programming autonomous [self-driving] vehicles.

F: I work with a team building an artificial intelligence system for autonomous vehicles. You probably see those cars driving with the cameras on their roofs? They navigate and snap billions of pictures as they move around the city.

F: We use all those data pictures to create artificial intelligence so that self-driving vehicles can [see] the roads and decide how to drive. They constantly take photos of the vehicle's surroundings, and the artificial intelligence software allows the car to respond appropriately. It is all guided by a supercomputer.

F: The AI software identifies fixed objects that inform the driving application. The AI distinguishes objects that can potentially move from fixed ones. That work alone takes tremendous computing power, operating at incredibly high speed, using tons of visual data.

Z: Yeah, AI technology has advanced over the last decade. It's not perfect yet, but you'll see our artificial intelligence programs working in all cars in the next few years.

F: Everyone's cars will become more connected.

M: Connected to what?

F: When a vehicle is 'connected,' it communicates with other devices, networks, and cars.

Z: Cars will talk to each other and send information to the supercomputer. A network of other computers analyzes all the car-camera picture data feeds for roads, signs, cars, obstacles, and people and builds a map.

Z: We teach the computer to detect various objects—ones that move and ones that don't.

M: Wow, that sounds cool.

F: Yeah, the network analyzes trillions of images per second, and then the AI software performs three primary functions: object detection, object labeling, and [distance] estimates.

Z: The neural network processes the video data from all the vehicle cameras and creates a birds-eye-view of the roads.

M: So, autonomous cars help build a map?

Z: Then the AI software locates all the stationary objects like buildings and trees and makes a 3D map like in the Matrix movies with an astonishing top-down view."

M: I am not sure how this works, but it sounds impressive. Do you guys think autonomous vehicles will put me as a Lyft driver out of business?

F: I think most people are confused about autonomous driving. I think it will be some time before we see fully autonomous vehicles on the roads, maybe ten years before there are fully autonomous Lyft vehicles.

Z: There are six levels of autonomous vehicles, ranging from level 0 (no autonomy) to level 5 (fully autonomous). Most of the vehicles we work on, and test are level 2, sometimes level 3 trying to get to the higher levels.

Z: However, the higher the level of autonomy, the greater the risk of cyber-attack. So, people don't know cybersecurity is essential to the artificial intelligence design and implementation processes to be as safe as possible.

F: There are multiple ways for autonomous vehicles to be connected. So, unfortunately, there are plenty of opportunities for hackers to exploit. Hackers look for weaknesses or bugs in the programming software and systems to find a way into it.

F: Once they find a way in, they may be able to do various things, from changing a car's radio station to taking control of the steering wheel. That is what scares all of us.

Z: Hackers will have even more opportunities to exploit vehicle systems vulnerabilities and launch attacks that don't depend on accessing a vehicle's software.

F: We are trying to find software engineers that can work like hackers and expose the vulnerabilities in AI.

M: I had no idea. I imagine the automotive industry is taking cybersecurity seriously so that we may all be safer on the roads.

M: What is a neural network, if you don't mind me asking?

F: A supercomputer that communicates with millions of smaller computers resembling a big computing brain. A neural network.

Z. Feng gets off talking about Tesla's supercomputers. He uses words that few people use, like petabytes which is a million billion. The supercomputer that we work with processes 640 terabytes per second, a lot of processing speed.

F: Tesla uses a neural network to operate a camera-based system. A neural network shares information with the entire network to 'learn' and become more efficient and effective.

M: We drive around using our vision and brains to process what we see into information we use to make decisions in our driving. We need a neural network system able to process visual input in large volumes and at a breakneck speed to replicate the depth and velocity of all the fixed and moving objects around us in real-time. Does that sound correct?

Z: Yes, exactly. The big question is: Can a computer-based neural network do the same thing as a human brain? And we think the answer is perhaps yes now because we have the vision processor capability with this new neural net. It is an exciting time.

F: While we as engineers are working to improve all the Self-Driving features, the software programming is being continuously tweaked and improved. Feng's team does some of the beta-testing. A few companies employ large teams of machine learning engineers working on the autonomous driving neural network. Each works on a small web component, plugging their results into the more extensive network.

Z: We have a team of roughly 20 people training neural networks full-time. They're all cooperating on a single neural network. It is a race to see who will get it up and running first."

F: This is why most self-driving car companies, including Alphabet's subsidiary Waymo, use lidars that use laser light to create 3D maps of the car's surroundings. It emits laser beams in all directions and computes the distances between fixed objects.

Z: Lidars can provide added information filling the information gaps in the neural networks.

M: It must be tough to create a precise mapping of every location the self-driving car will be traveling within.

F: At test time, we are localizing that map to drive around a small area. The lidar units [those cars with the lasers on their roofs] have to drive around and collect tons of data daily. It's difficult [and costly] to build and maintain a high-definition lidar map. We merely try and build out a small travel area [usually a smaller city] and see what kind of computer capacity it takes to keep it up to date.

F: Once we have pre-mapped the environment with the lidar, we can create a high-definition map using the neural network. Then we must insert all the driving lanes, figure out how they connect, and then insert all the traffic lights," It takes an army of programmers to do all this." We need more AI and a faster neural network to do this complex work.

****

The AI research seems cool from what they are telling us. There is one NFL team now using lidar with football players where the players each have a sensor in their helmets, and the lidar data produces a 3D map of the game. I am sure the video game designers love this idea.

Another one I just heard a rumor about is where they put sensors on Army soldiers in the field, and the data they collect creates real-time video maps of the battlefield. They also use drones to manage and update data, and coordinate battlefield tactics, soldier deployments, and weapons use practices.

I wonder if we are creating a surveillance state like China. Feng seems to think it will lead to all sorts of innovation. I fear that pretty soon, every person and every home appliance will be sending data to these supercomputers for AI analysis…what companies and governments do with all the data is anyone's guess. We are far from perfecting the technology, and the misuse of this technology has been at least partially responsible for a multitude of accidents. My Lyft passengers believed it was usually driver error causing all the problems. Of course, this story is from the software engineers!

I had many questions we didn't have time to discuss. For example, what happens when a driverless car gets pulled over by the police? I mean, who gets the ticket? Can driverless vehicles even get pulled over, or are they simply unplugged?

I believe there are still many autonomous-driving challenges to figure out. Nonetheless, what we were talking about was fascinating. What the technologies they are developing mean for society remains to be seen.

Some AI advancements seem workable, and others make people nervous. Technology is way ahead of what the average person encounters. Let's hope they exercise extreme caution and safety when operating these vehicles on today's roads.

I imagine Lyft [the company] is excited about the prospect of driver-less cars. It would eliminate one of the most considerable costs, the driver! We're still far from living in a world with fully autonomous Lyft vehicles everywhere. If we rush it and work out all the bugs, there is a good chance that many people will get hurt or killed.

Beyond the lab, there are many problems we have yet to solve. Self-driving technology has figured out where the driving lanes are, where the traffic lights are and whether they are red, yellow, or green at any given moment. However, generating real-time information about road conditions is a future goal. Vision-based autonomous driving is problematic because it requires broad and fast computing [neural networks] that function based on the receiving video data feeds. These massive feeds demand super-fast computing capacity.

These two young men seemed so open-eyed to the positive prospect of computer technology solving complex mobility problems. They are not alone in exuding great confidence while explaining and describing how autonomous vehicles work. Being a professor, I admitted my skepticism. Technology seems to be way ahead of ethical concerns. Some AI advancements are undoubtedly exciting, and many others make people nervous. Nonetheless, the problems they were talking about were technical.

Story Twenty-Two

Groceries and Dispensaries

October 19, 2021

How do You choose between personal health and personal pleasure? Can one person have both? There are two common destinations that I served as a Lyft driver beyond merely ferrying people to their various jobs. These two destinations are grocery stores and cannabis dispensaries. Most passengers I help tell me they cannot afford a vehicle, and I accept their argument. Owning [or leasing a car] is very expensive. I marveled at how many people I met struggled to decide whether to spend their money on the newly legalized cannabis products rather than good healthy food. A typical passenger was wrestling with her cannabis/grocery dilemma with an unusual attitude. My next passenger seemed very nervous. She got in and said, "I have two stops."

M: OK, no problem. I see the first stop is OZ Something or the Wizard of OCD?

P: Yeah, It's a cannabis dispensary. I must go there first. It only takes a few minutes. Going to the grocery store takes about an hour. I hate to admit it, but buying my weekly cannabis comes first now since my medical diagnosis, then I spend the rest of my money on groceries.

M: Oh, no judgment here.

P: The cannabis I use is for medical reasons. I had the covid-19 virus about six months ago. I got sick enough to be hospitalized for a week. Then I didn't feel right about a month later. I kept getting these migraine headaches, and then I had a seizure, so they decided to take a scan of my entire body. They found I had a small tumor in my brain, the size of an almond above the inside of my left ear.

P: They did tests and found out it was benign, which means it wasn't growing, but I am waiting for them to decide whether there will be surgery or radiation treatments. I am scared.

M: I can hardly imagine.

P: About three months ago, I was visiting my friend. She asked me if I had ever tried smoking marijuana for my headaches. She said medical marijuana was legal in Michigan for more than ten years.

M: I don't smoke marijuana.

P: Anyway, she gave me a joint to smoke, and damn if it didn't relieve my headache! I was surprised and wondered why I hadn't thought of it sooner. So, until they operate [or if they operate], I plan to use marijuana as a pain treatment. It works well but is expensive, and my insurance doesn't pay for it.

P: But I don't think I will be able to resume my old job. Ha ha. I was a stock manager at a local grocery store when all this started. I mean the pandemic. We must take a drug test before I can return to work, and now, I might not pass it. I am unsure if the company or the insurance will give me a waiver or a pass.

M: I know that many companies give new employees a drug test. They recommend you refrain from drug use a week before taking the test. I don't think Lyft requires such a test. I think it should test people that are going to drive others.

M: I would try and avoid any mix-up. I would inform your employer that you're on prescription meds while they take an oral swab to test your saliva for drugs. Doing so lets them know beforehand that you're on a medical prescription. You should also give them your physician's contact information so they can call to confirm that you're on a specific medical marijuana prescription.

M: They're not allowed to ask what you're taking or why you're taking it. Doctor-patient confidentiality protects your information. Unfortunately, you may have to get a lawyer if they reject the test results and terminate your employment.

P: Imagine having to choose between your medicine and your groceries? I am not sure I could even do my old job while high on cannabis. I feel spacy if I smoke. I get wiped out if I put it in my food. It wears off in a few hours, but then I feel tired. Sometimes I get a headache. There is no simple answer here.

****

The storyteller here was a grocery employee [stock manager]. She was one of my first duplicate riders. She worked for a Fortune 100 company with hundreds of stores. They have seven stores in the SE Michigan area where I Lyft drive. I take Lyft passengers to and from local grocery stores daily. I enjoy these rides because I get out of the car, walk around, and stretch my legs. I use the restroom. One of the first things I learned about Lyft driving was to know where you can walk around and use the public restroom facilities. I cannot emphasize the importance of understanding this.

The same passenger delivers two parts of the story on two separate rides about a week apart. The first was to the grocery store. The second was to the cannabis dispensary. The first part of the story is about the first couple of days as a manager, and the second part is about how the store employees [including managers] dealt with the pandemic.

They made her a manager because someone quit abruptly, and she had been one of their high-performing employees during the last year, mainly stocking the dairy and juice sections. She told me the vendors that supply various products do most of the initial stocking of the shelves, but during the night, we replenish the entire store before opening the next day.

The Rising Cannabis Industry in SE Michigan. Michigan's medical and recreational marijuana market continues to post record monthly numbers, with sales reaching $115.4 million in March, more than March 2020 (Detroit Free Press, March 2021).

Michigan's sales of cannabis have been robust since the state's adult-use market launched in 2019, totaling more than $520 million in the program's first full year. Headset predicts sales in Michigan will grow significantly in April 2022, with a likely boost from the 4/20/22 unofficial cannabis holiday (Headset, 2022).

Michigan currently has 275 recreational cannabis stores and 410 medical marijuana dispensaries, according to Detroit Metro Times (March 2022). This publication also noted that Michigan issued new permits in 2021 for 45 more recreational marijuana shops and 46 medical cannabis dispensaries. Let's hope Lyft drivers avoid smoking [or eating] cannabis while driving.

Story Twenty-Three

Foodies Unite

October 20, 2021

A woman wrestles with losing contact with her favorite friends during the pandemic. She is attempting to restore friendships. These Foodies are developing an innovative solution to reacquaint themselves and businesses isolated by the pandemic. Their Foodie adventures bring them together using Lyft rides to share the travel/ dining experience cost. This story taught me more about maintaining friendships during difficult times.

Occasionally, Lyft driving takes me quite a distance from my home zone in Ann Arbor. When that happens, I must filter my ride requests to return closer to home or, on occasion, get caught in what I earlier called a strange loop. Another strange loop is ride requests that keep me going in circles within a specific area for hours. Sometimes I think my entire life has been one unique collection of strange loops [I introduced this effect in a slightly different way in an earlier story].

I picked up a middle-aged woman ten miles north of my Ann Arbor/Ypsilanti zone. She was well-dressed and seemed very excited to be getting a Lyft ride.

M: Hello, where to?

P: Well, I am meeting my Foodie Group for a special meal in Ann Arbor. I have some special friends from out of town. I am meeting them at Zingerman's Roadhouse!

M: That sounds like fun.

P: Yes, this is the first time in a long time we have been able to dine in anywhere since the pandemic started. I thought all our favorite restaurants were going to close. I was so upset when Mikette closed. My Foodie pals were so depressed. Ann Arbor deserves some accolades because such places were becoming big-deal culinary destinations for us.

M: Yes, I am familiar with it. Mikette sure was a charming little "French" Bistro in Ann Arbor. Yes, we have sidewalk cafes and quirky food trucks too. How many plant-based and gluten-free diners do you have in your city?

What makes Ann Arbor's food culture so strong and varied? An overall trend toward healthier lifestyles is part of it. Another part is the influx of faculty and students from all over the world interested in exploring other cuisines while maintaining their ethnic and cultural preferences.

P: It has been so rough on restaurants and their regular patrons. When someone gets enthusiastic about doing something, it lifts everybody else. There are opportunities for everybody."

P: Everyone knows about Zingerman's deli, yet not everyone knows they also run a creamery, a bakery, and two full-service restaurants. To me, Zingerman's is synonymous with good eating.

M: I know their history; what started as a tiny corner delicatessen back in 1982 by friends Ari Weinzweig and Paul Saginaw grew into a family of more than a dozen food-related businesses.

P: My Foodie adventures always start with them and continue when I bring people to Ann Arbor. A Community of Businesses joins the deli and its much-heralded Reuben sandwich on hand-sliced Jewish rye.

M: They are one of the Top 5 employers in Ann Arbor.

P: It gets better. My Foodie group regularly meets at Zingerman's Roadhouse restaurant. They launched with Chef Alex Young, a 2011 James Beard Foundation award-winner whose creations feature American regional food.

P: Their menu included buttermilk-fried chicken, roasted red peppers, macaroni, and cheese. Dessert was a decadent homemade Dutch donut with vanilla gelato lathered with bourbon-caramel sauce and crowned with a black cherry. What impresses us as foodies is their chef's passion for local agriculture, and natural foods inspired his "chef's garden," where the produce grown shows up on the plates of Roadhouse dinners. What's in the garden? "Just about any vegetable that grows in Michigan.

P: Another great Foodie destination is the upscale Grange Kitchen & Bar. The owner strives to serve only food grown and produced within 50 miles of Ann Arbor. He shops at the farmers' markets, getting produce directly from local growers for his seasonal menus. He makes sausage, too! The upstairs bar features bacon-infused bourbon, orange bitters, and in-house brandied cherries.

P: Staying local is the attraction for the Foodie element. The pandemic has made it more accessible in recent years due to the increased number of farmers and growers experimenting with longer growing seasons and niche crops.

M: My favorite is an Ann Arbor institution, the Fleetwood Diner, which calls itself the "hippest little diner." The classic small aluminum-sided restaurant that looks like a railcar, built from a kit in 1948 and open 24 hours, is a longtime hit with UM students and A2 locals alike. Fleetwood Grill's signature Hippie Hash is a mélange of homemade hash browns topped with grilled tomato, green pepper, onion, mushroom, broccoli, and feta cheese.

M: Oh, and the other small jewel is Ayse's Turkish Cafe, a homey sit-down and carry-out restaurant.

M: The challenge is it's hidden in the back of a strip mall on A2's north side, but Ayse's loyal following knows how to find her. She does all the cooking herself, often making up the menus on the fly depending on what's available at her next-door butcher and the farmer's market. Her lentil soup is a unique local favorite, and the allspice cinnamon chicken is fantastic. I am starting to sound like a commercial.

P: We took the Foodie group to the Taste Kitchen for a sophisticated fusion of Asian, French, and American dishes made from local produce and sustainably sourced seafood. Vietnamese-born Danny Van is both chef and artist who layers his flavors with imagination and flair. I still can taste the crab and curry butternut squash soup.

M: I am getting hungry!

P: Did I mention Mikette Bistro & Bar, described by owner Adam Baru as a "French-ish bistro." The atmosphere is casual, and the food is Southern French comfort food. It was more rustic than traditional cooking with beef bourguignon, roasted chicken and salmon, and pates that got raves. Sadly, the pandemic claimed this gem as a casualty.

P: Being a Foodie is not about eating much at all. It is about the shared experience of dining and eating fantastic food with friends.

M: Where do I sign up?

****

People use Lyft in such innovative ways. The Foodies I met get six couples together to meet at some restaurant or wine-tasting vineyards, like a MeetUp, and they all take a Lyft ride. What is remarkable about how they do the actual rideshare is that they all end up paying the exact cost for the ride AND the meals…because they figure it out that way…so there is NO advantage or disadvantage to choosing a destination.

Ann Arbor, Michigan, is not just for college football! Ann Arbor is a dream destination for foodies, too! A robust and diverse foodie scene, Ann Arbor/Ypsilanti boasts nearly 320 area restaurants–from townie favorites to world-class eateries–where international flavors blend with a strong farm-to-table ideology.

I spoke to a few restaurant owners in A2 about all the business closures. It turns out that many of the chain restaurants received federal loans and aid dollars while small independents got nothing. So many restaurants that made Ypsilanti and Ann Arbor special were closed for at least six months in 2020 and 3-4 more months on average during 2021.

Do we need more generic chain restaurants and fast-food drive-thru's? Who takes their Foodie group to Applebee's? There were some Foodies in Ypsilanti that I would take to Depot Town or the many historical Coney Islands, yet Ann Arbor is a much larger and wealthier city. The restaurants are varied and more international, serving a larger University complex, and its residents enjoy its world-class cuisine.

Some more pleasurable rides involved picking up couples in Ann Arbor and Ypsilanti, going out for an early evening meal, or celebrating some special family occasion. I asked them, "Why do you use Lyft to travel locally?" They all owned cars yet preferred to go out using quick Lyft rides instead of paying for parking and navigating the downtown area at night during the busy periods. They celebrate [and drink] to their heart's content without worrying about driving home. I found this out during my first Surprise Foodie Birthday!

I mentioned that a new restaurant had opened near my home called the Dixboro project. They have a Michelin chef and an outstanding menu. I encourage your foodie group to explore this amazing restaurant in NE Ann Arbor.

Story Twenty-Four

Consecutive and Duplicates

October 21, 2021

This is a story about some regular driving patterns that I observed. The first is consecutive rides where two back-to-back go to the same destination. The second I call Duplicates, where a single passenger experiences multiple rides, sometimes on the same day [Dr. Jekyll Meets Mr. Hyde]. My next duplicate ride occurred a little after three weeks of driving. She didn't remember riding with me. She got into my car and said hello, but quickly returned to her phone. I immediately thought I recognized the exact pick-up location as one I had been to a few days, perhaps a week prior, but I wasn't sure. I thought it would go a bit differently if I picked up someone for a second time. Halfway through the ride my passenger looked up and said:

P: Hey, I know you! You're the Lyft driver writing that book. How's it coming along?

M: Yes, that's right. Good. I am making steady progress.

P: Am I in your book? When will it be published? I told everyone about your book last week. Could you share an update with us?

M: Well, you are the first duplicate rider I have had ever.

P: What was the title of your book again. Does everybody use Lyft? I thought you were making up that story to entertain your passengers. Here is my stop. Right here.

M: Hmmm. That was strange. I don't expect to engage everyone. Some people couldn't care less about what I shared! No matter. Push the Last Ride button.

Next I picked up a couple at the A2 Train Station on my next ride. They were in for the weekend from Chicago, staying in an Airbnb and meeting some friends the next day. I remember telling them I was familiar with Airbnb because I picked up the owner. I told them it was a good one, and they seemed pleased. Another strange coincidence was that the Airbnb was also right inside the area where I got lost recently with all the construction barricades. I was a bit nervous because it was getting dark, and I didn't want to repeat that nightmare.

P: Hi. Matt. Good to meet you. I'm Jerry, and this is Megan. You said you know this Airbnb?

M: Yes, sir, I picked up the owner last week, and we had a great chat.

P: We thought we would try it out. Our friends are coming into town later tonight. I don't know where they are staying. They are coming from Pittsburgh. We are all UM alums. We try and get together in A2 every year. Last year we all had to cancel.

M: That's great. Most of the restaurants and pubs are open again.

I picked up another couple the following day whose destination happened to be the same Airbnb address. They said they had to stay in a "not-so-nice" motel in A2. They made a morning Lyft ride request to meet their friends. Their friends were the ones I drove to the Airbnb the evening before! They were so surprised at how easily I found the house after their friends [my previous passengers] told them how difficult a time I had. Familiarity erases possible surprises. It was a coincidence picking up both couples on two consecutive days on two successive rides [the last ride one day and my first ride on the next]. The only "consecutive" ride that stood out beyond the Airbnb couples visiting A2 was picking up a restaurant server for one Downtown A2 restaurant immediately after picking up a couple going to that same restaurant. For some strange reason, that coincidence didn't seem so unusual.

I didn't get another duplicate rider until Day 28, October 24 - strange effects of duplication and repeats in my Lyft network. I thought there would be more frequent duplicates. I would argue that my network is too small.

The simplest way to suggest organizing is to repeat. Consecutives are distinct from duplicates because they occur when separate consecutive riders go to the same destination (ex. Sporting events or church service] or return to the same pick-up address as the previous ride. These certainly may seem like fortunate accidents or coincidences of the rarest kind. Repetition can be intentional or surprising. Either way, it influences how organizing occurs.

I see some strange patterns in the multiple rides and routes. These redundant paths and more familiar "duplicate passengers" lead to questioning my random [unconscious] travel choices and [conscious] driving habits that limit surprises I experience. In some rare cases, they do the opposite and produce a sense of uncertainty. I am always wondering how these ride patterns could help me understand organizing.

Story Twenty-Five

Ghost in the Machine

October 22, 2021

"The [challenging problem] is how our amazing private world of human consciousness emerges from the material world. How can we make sense of the magic and mystery of life without an appeal to the supernatural is the challenge? Science has not adequately answered this challenge. There is still a ghost in the machine."

-Owen Flanagan

I needed to tell one of my own stories to a gracious Lyft passenger (Dr. Herman, a UM faculty colleague) who asked me. So, on the twenty-fifth day of driving, I did. As a graduate student at Michigan for eight years, people more intelligent than myself surrounded me. All were trying to solve the most complex problems. I struggled to understand those problems.

I was fortunate to take a few courses in a department called the Center for the Study of Complex Systems (CSCS). It was an eclectic mix of scientists [natural and social] pulled together by a group of brilliant UM professors, one of whom served on my dissertation committee. He became one of my most influential mentors. His name was Michael D. Cohen, and this is my homage to one of the finest thinkers of our time and a true inspiration. As told by one of Dr. Cohen's closest associates, the rest was my experience.

Exploring organizing as a verb was the essence of my dissertation and corresponded to Dr. Cohen's advice that what I inferred was a high-velocity organization (HVO). One of the most vital exemplars of HVO was UM's Residential College (RC), where the concept of familiarity explained how the RC worked.

People familiar with multiple languages and cultures quickly joined [organized] college-level education programs in weeks, evolving into an independent college. You could never actually see the RC because it changed all the time.

The high-velocity organizing concept originates in the assumption that organizations never exist in any form of stasis [mistakenly lending themselves to be defined and identified as nouns]. Organizations are always enactments best described as "verbs" dynamic interactions subject to constant change [emergent] and complexity [variation influenced by multiple causations. Organizing is equifinal, meaning they exhibit varied become and, in turn, "be"]. It is about how volatile and chaotic they evolve and devolve in observable change—heady stuff that Karl Weick first charted.

The fundamental question in the organizational study is not about what makes organizations appear to be stable "things or nouns" [a discernable organization as an object]. This is the question that Cohen and Peterson helped me form. However, most of the research on organization study focused on how much "things grow and persist "-a significant error in the organization ontology [being]. I would need more time and energy to explain this adequately.

The problem posed in my dissertation was: How does [organizing] change in appearance cause us to treat it as [evolving/devolving?] using various measures [4-Rs]? Do we have the right tools or adequate observable lenses to gather evidence? You are probably wondering what does this have to do with Lyft driving? I want to know if gig work is HVO.

Dr. Cohen told me how he came to computer science and the study of information theory back in the late 1960s as he worked with John Holland, Robert Axelrod, and Arthur Burks. He knew all about the BACH group at UM because he [the C in BACH] was a founding member.

I took Dr. Herman to the Apple Store at the Briarwood Mall, where he was having some computer equipment checked. He was hard of hearing, 82 years old, and still working at the University.

P: Could you imagine having a robot as a colleague? The idea may seem rather fanciful. But, according to Dr. Cohen, we are witnessing a rise in the Autonomous World. The digital transformation of everything drives the Autonomous World. "It relies on the merger of robots and The Internet of Things (IoT)," It is already creating new ways of doing business. It is also changing the Sharing Economy in numerous ways [rideshare].

Michael Cohen also introduced me to the Small Worlds and Six Degrees of Separation phenomena (and UM professor Duncan Watts) and Scott Page, who is another expert in complexity. His book, The Difference is original and a most fascinating read!

M: Dr. Herman, you told me that your best friend and most influential colleague at Michigan was Michael D. Cohen.

P: Is that right? Well, there were two major influences.
.

M: I happened to be one of Dr. Cohen's doctoral students in the late 1990s. He was one of my two doctoral advisors, Marvin Peterson was my department chair, and Michael Cohen co-chaired my dissertation committee with Marvin W. Peterson. Both were [generous mentors] during my entire UM eight-year tenure as a graduate student.

They both guided my interest in organizational dynamics. Let me tell you a story about Michael Cohen, and then I will tell you one about Marvin Peterson.

When I was a third-year graduate student at Michigan, Dr. Cohen gave me a challenge. He asked me to go and collect a couple of hundred citations [800] on organizational learning,

M: He told me it would serve me well in contemplating a dissertation project and perhaps lead to writing a literature review for a proposed journal article.

M: I remember telling Dr. Peterson about this academic "chore," as he called it. He laughed and told me, "It figures he would give you an impossibly laborious chore to see if you are serious. I mean, see what you come up with."

M: I first went to talk to another respected voice in our field, the Rensis Likert professor of organizational behavior, Karl Weick, and he thought the chore was a great idea. "This will keep you busy and could lead to writing something original." He was right.

M: So, I found around 820 citations covering much territory from evolutionary biology and ecology, physics and mechanics, mathematics, game theory, and this new academic field called "complexity science." It took me four months to find that number of citations and filter out all the irrelevant ones. There were many areas in this list where I had very little knowledge. I read incessantly. However, the sheer breadth of topics was astonishing and overwhelming. They piqued my curiosity, yet I struggled to keep it all together. I felt it was getting all mixed up in my mind. Michael Cohen said. "That's good. Keep reading."

M: I turned in this stack of citations to Dr. Cohen said he would scan through them and get back to me. He did so in about a week and said, "Are you ready for phase 2?" I said sure. "Now, listen carefully because this will be a challenge." He said in a serious tone. "I want you to select 85 or so of the best articles noted in your list…here are the criteria for selection." He gave me a note sheet with four statements on it. I read them out and looked up. "Do you have any questions about this assignment or the statements on that sheet? No, sir. I said.

M: Have at it, and once you have the eighty-five, I want you to read each article and write a 750–800-word annotation. Then we will get together and talk more. See you before the spring semester ends. I figured out that would be nearly 65,000 words, enough for a book.

M: I taught three courses that semester. I kept having to postpone our meeting, but I kept Dr. Cohen updated on my progress. It was a stressful assignment on top of all my other studies. I asked a lot of other professors about specific articles, even contacting some article authors for suggestions and related articles. It was hard work. I thought I would never finish it. But I did around mid-July.

M: I remember slipping this 250-page collection of annotations under Dr. Cohen's office door, and it was a good thing his door had a two-inch space underneath it. I laughed, thinking he had the door trimmed so students could return borrowed books by shoving them under the door. He had the most fantastic library. I took a photo of it.

M: About three weeks went by. I received an email summoning me to his faculty office. I arrived early. He answered his door and said, "Let's go and get a coffee. OK, with you?" I wasn't sure we needed any coffee at 3:00 pm. We walked briskly, and he seemed very energized. He told me he had finished reading the annotations.

We sat down, and he first said he wanted to know what I thought of the challenge and how I managed it, and then he asked me specific questions designed to draw what I thought.

OK, I said. There is something that I have been thinking a lot about, yet I am no expert. I read a lot of journal articles and a few books. I took some notes. I began thinking about how complicated studying what organizing is. Dr. Peterson told me early on that we already have a huge error in our field that creates much confusion, and that is we tend to think of an organization as a noun rather than a verb, meaning organizing. There is no such "thing" as an organization."

You know that criticism of our field originates with Karl Weick's work. He was one the first to level this charge. Wow, I didn't know that. Go on.

Here is what I began to think. Perhaps we misuse the term organization (as a noun) because we as humans tend to reify [take abstract ideas and make them more concrete, thinking them as more real]. Exactly, go on.

Look at all this research that attempts to describe and explain human organizations, churches, schools, companies, governments, nations, etc. If they were "things" or nouns, we seem singularly concerned by what we believe holds them together over time as if they were solid objects or parts of the physical space beyond their buildings or artifice. Interesting.

So, it seems that we are likely to fall into line in this field and study how "organizations" evolve [persist] toward emulating not abstractions or verbs but something more persistent and concrete. Otherwise, we deem them failures or irrelevant simply because they do not survive. After reading all this material, I want to learn how organizing [as a verb] operates…I want to know about organizing velocity [verb speed] or the dynamics of organizing. I want to learn why certain forms of organizing persist and others do not. I am curious about the idea: I want to see if I can find high-velocity organizing where human "organizing" evolves and devolves quickly.

Instead of focusing on organizations such as the Catholic Church or the Icelandic Parliament, I want to learn about more verbs that appear and disappear intentionally and swiftly. Not because they are failures or seek to persist over time, but because this organizing will define part of the future. I don't know how— [from a conversation in 1998].

Marv Peterson looked at the set of annotations. He said, Matt, you need to write your paper from this, Matt, as a possible proposal for your dissertation. I think this has the makings of a novel idea. It may be essential to extend and flesh it out. I will help you. In the meantime, you have put much effort into this, you are a candidate in our department, and I want to extend an offer to redo your comprehensive exams instead of using this work as a dissertation proposal.

Both professors were gracious and pushed me way beyond imagination. I wrote a research paper on my so-called big idea about "high-velocity" organizing and submitted it to a conference for the first time. That summer, I was invited to present my paper at the Academy of Management in Boston, MA. My wife even took me to an equally exciting Red Sox baseball game.

I must tell you about the experience of giving my first academic talk at Harvard Business School to about 300 people. My advisors: Karl Weick, Marvin Peterson, Robert Quinn, Jane Dutton, and Michael Cohen, were present. I am sure they don't remember. It also seemed like the UM Ross School of Business was in attendance.

The room was packed, and I was the third speaker up. And as I approached the podium, Karl Weick was just behind me. People were quietly applauding. Then Michael Cohen came to introduce me and stopped just short he said, are you nervous? That is OK. Act natural. Take a deep breath and take your time.

He introduced me. Then I made a rookie mistake. I started to recognize people in the audience, especially those I cited in the paper. Dr. Cohen looked at me. He leaned over toward me, put his hand over his mouth, and said, look, this is an organization like any other noun. The audience makes the place seem more of a noun than a verb. It just looks like a church to inspire permanence and reverence.

Matt, at this moment, YOU are the expert for a few moments because NO ONE here has spent more time thinking, studying, and writing about this topic than you have. All you must do is restart the conversation, you have this great new idea, and they all want to hear about it mainly because it will reawaken their interest in things they haven't focused on for years. Take a few questions, and when you have finished, I will come up and join you. I will grab your elbow, and you can relax and move off to the side. I will field some questions with you and let you go.

I managed to get through the presentation OK, but then a slew of questions hit me like darts. I tried to answer first by complimenting audience members on their astute observations and keen insights. Dr. Cohen did approach the podium after about ten minutes. He did grab my elbow and never let it go. He almost did and then looked at me and winked. When it was over, a group of about twenty graduate students pinned me up against the wall asking for a hard copy of the paper.

Later that evening, I joined Dr. Cohen, Marv Peterson, and a few other professors for tea at the Charles Hotel in Cambridge, MA. Marv was a Harvard alum, so he knew everything about the place. During the conversation, Dr. Cohen decided to embarrass me a bit more. He announced to the group that I was joining the faculty ranks, albeit short of the Ph. D. and not quite a candidate, as an instructor at the University of Tulsa. They applauded, which made me feel even more out of place.

After the fun moment, and as the other professors resumed their side conversations, Dr. Cohen leaned over to me and said, "Now, when you graduate with your doctorate, I am confident this will happen. I want YOU to be the hand on the elbow of your students. You will do fine work, Matt, and they will learn many important things from you as I have."

****

A few years later, I defended my dissertation, guided in some measure by my "high velocity" organizing idea. I still have the original paper I wrote back in 1998 on the subject. It was probably my best research effort as a graduate student.

I finished my presentation, and Dr. Cohen came up and said, "Do you have a few minutes? I would appreciate spending a little time telling you everything I learned from you over the last few years." What an amazingly generous overture by such an esteemed professor? I was thrilled and accepted enthusiastically. It was one of the most humbling and uplifting conversations ever.

Dr. Cohen said near the end of our talk, "And by the way, I need to thank another of my advisors, Marvin Peterson. You may not know it, but Marv was one of your biggest advocates behind the scenes." He may not have told you much about how he helped you, and that is how he is, but his consistent [and relentless] support for you with other faculty, including myself, was highly influential. He convincingly recommended you for that first teaching assignment in the Information Science program I led, even though he couldn't help you directly with any typical TA/RA opportunities.

My doctoral experience at Michigan was a serious eight-year ordeal due to lack of funding, not generating a viable research agenda, and my academic shortfalls. In many ways, I was way over my head, but I have grit. I believed in serendipity, those fortunate accidents that occur when you never give up. I graduated from one of the prestigious Universities on the planet, the first in my entire family to do so. Every time I visit my old Detroit neighborhood while Lyft driving, I think about how far I traveled, how hard I worked, and how grateful I am to be where I am today.

Sadly, Michael D. Cohen, complexity theorist, UM Ford School of Public Policy, founding member of the School of Information, mentor, friend, and the most amazing teacher and human being, unfortunately, passed away in 2013.

Story Twenty-Six

Lost in My Backyard

October 23, 2021

"Somehow, I strayed and lost my way, and now there'll be no time to play, no time for joy, no time for friends– not even time to make amends."
                    - Lewis Carroll, from Alice in Wonderland

We all find ourselves lost at one time or another. What we do when we feel lost sets the stage for meaningful learning. Confusion and humor come with feeling lost, yet patience and good humor return us to a sense of normality. Morgan was a middle-aged woman, and she was going out to visit a friend. She told me that she hadn't been out much over the past few months. She worked from home. Her friend agreed that now that they were both vaccinated, they could visit them in person. Their weekly Zoom call would still happen, yet they were both itching to get out of the house. It was getting dark, and her friend only lived a few miles away.

This Lyft ride started pleasant enough. I picked up Morgan in a familiar residential neighborhood in Ann Arbor, about half a mile from the UM campus after dark.

M: Hello, my name is Matt, and welcome to my 8th day as a Lyft driver!

P: It is your twenty-fifth-day driving, huh? Are you counting the days toward the end or saying that for fun?

M: No, it is my fourth week. I took one day off to rest. I am collecting passenger stories for a book-writing project.

P: Hmmm. That sounds fascinating. I don't have a good story for you. However, I am an elementary school teacher [fifth grade]. Things have been topsy-turvy since last spring.

M: That sounds like a great job. I bet the kids are tired of the pandemic.

P: Yes, they are tired of wearing masks, but I think they are tired of studying online from home too. They like recess the most, but they must stay six feet apart. I need a recess holiday myself.

M: Me, too. I must get out of this car every 30-45 minutes because driving is hard on my back and shoulders.

Morgan was very animated and excited to be out and about as she described the reason for her delight. I forgot to hit the pickup button on the app. Then when I did, off we were. Because I was tired, I remember the relief that we were staying in Ann Arbor.

The ride started OK. Surprisingly, we talked about writing projects. Morgan was meeting a friend who only lived about a half-mile from where I picked her up. We had to navigate through the neighborhood because road construction was on every street, blocking nearly all local intersections. A few strange things happened to us as we made our way: I missed the first turn; then I tried and doubled back, entering the construction zone. The GPS doesn't include the construction zones, so it plots a course as usual without the updated information about construction obstacles.

We retraced our route to try and get out another way. We wound through the same path twice and came to another dead end. We went around in circles, but at first, Morgan was having some fun trying to solve our route mishap. We passed her friend's house. She was standing on her porch looking for us, but Morgan and I missed her because we were so obsessed with looking at our phones.

They called each other and laughed because we were on her street, had passed her house, and didn't know. I was so tired, having driven around for twenty minutes in circles, turning what should have been a five-minute ride into a thirty-minute contest.

They started laughing when Morgan stood outside my car, telling her friend Susan about how lost we were [just a few blocks away]. Then I hit the drop-off button, showing that I made $3.27 for the ride. They started laughing. Privately, I felt cheated. Morgan also stopped laughing abruptly. She offered to pay me $5.00 more or give me a tip.

M: No need. At least it paid for the gas I burned.

P: I haven't laughed this hard in weeks.

M: OK, well then that was worth it.

So, I hit the button to continue, and there was no ride request. I was relieved. I waved at Morgan and her friend and went down the street. Hmmm, which way did I turn to get out of here? OK, right, yeah, right it is.

Wouldn't you know it, I went down the street and ended up at another dead end! I couldn't call Morgan and tell her, so I called my wife. Of course, she said to stay there, and I will pull up a map. No need, I will go back.

My wife Mia said: That might not help because the construction sites are not on the GPS. On the next try, I found my way out. I was exhausted and decided to call it a day. I wondered if other people had the same problem. How could the construction guys create this maze with only one way out?

****

I thought about calling the city offices and finding out how this occurred. Then I thought I would go to that same neighborhood in the daytime and see if the construction barriers were still there.

Most of the barricades were still there, and a few had toppled over! I wasn't the only one trapped that night by the construction "Road Closed" barriers. I thought of my old passenger who would have barreled through the barricades.

I tried to find the intersection where it had started. I turned in exactly where I saw the first road-closed barricades. I went down the first street until it ended at another barrier. I turned around and took the next road down three blocks until it ended. I wondered what the people living on these streets thought about the construction blockade. I saw a man sweeping the leaves from his driveway, so I decided to ask him about the barricades.

He told me, "Most of the barricades go up at the beginning of the workday when they must forget to remove them…so we move them aside. I wanted the streets fixed. We have been waiting for some of this roadwork to happen for a few years. It is worth the hassle." I told him about what happened to me last night. He stared at me with a puzzled look.

Why didn't I simply get out of your car and move them aside? Hmmm. I don't know. I felt confused and silly, like a lost kid, but lost in my backyard.

Story Twenty-Seven

Map Matching Mayhem

October 24, 2021

Sometimes the technology assisting you does not work no matter what you do. It is no one's fault. There is no one to blame. Technology is not error-free and 100% reliable despite engineers' confidence. I began the driving day mid-morning, later than usual. This tale of technology failure demands creative problem-solving. It takes a little grit to exercise some human discretion and compassion to do the right thing above and beyond what is expected or supported by technology.

My third fare was a pickup at the UM Hospital. When I arrived, the GPS told me to go to the Emergency entrance (The Security Guard later told me it always does), yet the pickup was at the Main Hospital entrance. I got into a long queue and waited to park just past the doors. I received a text message. A message from Lyft support told me that the passenger/customer was at the entrance to the Oncology Center a few doors down the street.

The message included a description of the waiting passenger. I skimmed it because I knew it would disappear in ten seconds. I remember thinking, this is the first human message I have heard from Lyft since I started this adventure. I had yet to interact with another human being at Lyft. Not during the entire sign-up or starter driver experience did I speak to anyone directly from the company I worked for, and this was profound and strange.

Everything had gone smoothly, and I thought I had figured things out well thus far. Little did I know that this day would be different. They say that you MUST make mistakes to learn big new lessons...well, today would be that first BIG Lyft lesson.

I picked up Mona at the Main Hospital Entrance [Mona - disguised name]. A one-half mile into the ride, the Lyft phone application informed me that I had completed the current ride.

Mona was still my passenger. We were hardly anywhere near her destination. She told me she was about thirty miles away. Mona was pleasant enough as I told her I would have to pull over and reset the ride.

I tried asking for HELP. The Lyft application keeps telling me that I cannot adjust my last ride. I didn't care about my earnings so much as I wanted to get Mona home promptly. I asked for help, but I could not get through to anyone. I sent multiple help messages to a Chat Bot that did not seem to understand ANY of my requests. It was frustrating, and I kept apologizing to the passenger for the delay. She even tried to re-request the ride to no avail.

I was stuck and decided to drive Mona home and deal with the problem with Lyft later. I drove Mona home, and she was pleased with the pleasant ride. We had a good chat. What should have taken 45 minutes round trip took almost two and a half hours. It was exhausting.

I had only clocked $30 in ride fares so far that day, so I decided to go home and record this incident rather than continue driving feeling so tired and frustrated.

The problem is that when facing human problems occurring while driving, I have almost no human support.

There is an AI Chat Bot that misunderstands me as much as it comprehends what I am requesting. The messages are impersonal and generic. They reminded me immediately that I was not having a conversational exchange with a human being.

M:I was interacting with a computer program! Then the result is an apology for any "inconvenience" sent from the AI working Lyft support chatbots.

M: More about the exchange [Directly from the Help Support CHAT (H) that begins at 10:42 am. My responses to Lyft Support are in italics]

H: Please describe your issue. I ended the ride by mistake [I wasn't sure what caused it to end, so I assumed it was something I did wrong]. Someone will respond in the next few minutes

H: Hello, Matthew. Thank you for contacting Lyft support. My name is May.

H: May I know which ride you are referring to?

   The one to Southfield MI
   It ended too early

M: The ride needs to be re-continued, and I don't know how to reset it. The passenger is with me. The destination is about 40 miles away.

   H. You should ask your passenger to enter destination changes in their app so we can track the entire ride. If you accidentally send a ride early, you should ask your passenger to re-request the ride so you can complete the ride on the platform. Learn more about Driver Pay http://www.lyft.driver/pay

H: Lyft does not issue earnings for any ride or portion of a ride completed off-platform.

I don't care about the earnings right now. I need help re-entering the ride.

H: This is a MUST, Matthew.

I don't understand how to do this.

H: If you give the rider an untracked ride, we cannot pay you.

H: Please have the rider re-request the ride.

That is wrong. I have a ride that Lyft ended incorrectly.

We haven't gotten to the destination. It told me the ride was completed [$4.12 was the incorrect earnings]

H: This was the rider, Noopuh?

M: No, that was the previous passenger!

H: Are you still with the first passenger?

M: Yes, I still have Mona in my car. We only got about a mile from the point of origin, and the computer said I had completed the ride.

H: I see that you had another ride after Mona?

M: No, that is wrong. Mona was after Noopur. I need to continue the ride to Southfield for Mona.

H: As mentioned, if you want to continue the ride with Mona, she must re-request the ride.

M: I asked Mona, and she re-requested the ride through her insurance company.

M: I am still with the rider now. She told me that another driver might provide the new ride.

H: Thank You for the Update. Have a Safe Ride.

H: If you have any need for additional assistance, please feel free to reach out to us at any time.

M: I have not received the re-requested ride, and neither has my rider.

M: Please have someone call me. The rider is confused, and so am I.

   Help? Help?

H: We know that some topics are easier to discuss on the phone.

H: While Lyft offers outreach support for a few common issue types, we don't have a direct phone number to call for driver support.

M: Please have someone call me. They called to tell me where the rider was. Why can't I speak to someone when I can't seem to resolve this issue? (I entered my cell number)

H: Matthew, Have Mona re-enter the request for a ride again. That is the only way we can track your ride with her app.

M: She did that. Now, I need help because it didn't show up.

H: You may proceed to your destination. I am unable to do outbound calls. I am sorry. I believe I have answered all your questions for today. I will be ending this chat if you don't have any other concerns besides this.

M: I turned to Mona and said, I will have to give you a ride home for free because Lyft isn't helping us resolve this issue. I am sorry, but on the bright side, your ride home only cost $4.12, and the rest is on me. I will have to take this up with Lyft later.

I dropped off Mona at her apartment and decided to call it a day.

****

It was a confusing experience. I had driven for twenty-five days and had never confronted this sort of problem. I felt embarrassed by this situation. I also felt humiliated that I confused my passenger. What started as amusing got very frustrating very fast. I was reminded of the experience on Day five with the Indian woman I picked up at the same hospital. I thought I knew the process.

I realize now how it all happened. When you are tired, you repeat mistakes and think you are doing things differently. Fatigue can make you feel a little insane. You think the world around you isn't working.

Not everyone requests their Lyft rides. On occasion, passengers have a surrogate ride requester. It is funny, but when someone gets in my car, and I hear a different name, I immediately think [they] have made an error. I never even consider that the Lyft platform is giving me a surrogate. I treat it as bogus information.

For example, discharged people requesting a ride from the hospital will often have a social worker or nurse order a Lyft ride. This process can significantly slow down the pickup process. The patient usually must wait to be wheeled to the hospital exit a few minutes after the requester orders the Lyft ride. I sit and remain beyond what the platform tells me, and then when the wait time is up, I am free to leave with no penalty or passenger. Yet, at the hospital, everything is a bit different. It took some time to understand this.

I had forgotten that this was standard hospital protocol for them (remember Story Five?]. I often waited for a rider upwards of fifteen minutes at the hospital entrance and was asked to move on to let other cars enter or exit. It was all extremely confusing. I would avoid taking hospital rides until I figured out how things worked. I don't believe I ever really did.

I wondered if I had had someone at Lyft to speak directly with and how swiftly we might have solved the problem. Instead, I had to endure the confusion of communicating with a chatbot.

Story Twenty-Eight

Tweedles

October 25, 2021

Silence can be unnerving, yet unbridled noise can unravel a person.

> "The time has come," the Walrus said,
> "To talk of many things:
> Of shoes—and ships—and sealing wax—
> Of cabbages—and kings—
> And why the sea is boiling hot-
> And whether pigs have wings."
>
> - Lewis Carroll

I picked up two young Indian women at one of the many new high-rise apartment buildings recently built in downtown Ann Arbor. These 12-15 story apartment buildings house wealthier UM students and are price-prohibitive for most A2 residents. I gave two young women the longest ride of the Lyft driving odyssey. The ride length was not aggravating. What made me go crazy was that they NEVER stopped talking. They were both on separate calls when they got into the back seat of my car. One told me we were going to Great Lakes Crossing, an outlet mall about 60 miles away. At first, I didn't know where or what the place was. They both seemed annoyed by my ignorance.

P: Follow the GPS! One of them chimed rather condescendingly. It is an outlet mall. Don't you know it? Everyone I know shops there!

M: I do know it, but I have never been there. Let me see where it is on GPS.

They began talking to each other by finishing each other's

sentences. They spoke English yet switched to speaking Hindi whenever they wanted to exclude me. I imagined there were parts of their conversation that they wanted to remain private. Suddenly, my car became a noisy call center.

However, when I asked them a direct question, one would answer in a commanding tone, and then the other would attempt to soften the answer by removing the first one's demeaning manner. They spoke to me as if talking to a servant. It was disconcerting to me and bordered on rudeness. The Hindi word for idiot is "muurkh," with a strong r sound. In slang, among friends, people would say "ulluu," -- which means owl, and in South Asian culture, denotes foolishness.

P: We are busy getting purchase orders from our friends back in India. They buy all sorts of things from us via StockX. Mostly they buy sneakers and cosmetics they cannot find in India.

M: I don't know StockX. How does it work?

P: StockX is a resale platform. We post a pair of hot sneakers that we mark up sometimes 200%, and the fools back home pay the high for them. They pay for the shipping cost too. They want the latest from America. They want to appear rich, and some are rich.

P: Yeah, we make enough to pay for college. She doesn't have to because her dad is rich. He taught us how to do it.

M: Don't you feel guilty that you are exploiting your friends like this?

P: No, because if we didn't do it, someone else would. Some of these sneakers go for a thousand dollars or more.

M: That is a reasonable justification for gouging people? For God's sake, some proper business ethics. I am a retired business professor with a Ph. D. from UM.

They immediately changed their tone, which I found strange. After another brief apology, they returned to business conversations in Hindi, floating effortlessly from boy troubles, the envy of close friends, to selling various clothing, shoes, and cosmetics to their customers back in India.

P: No, the Lancome Absolue is $425, and the new Air Jordan 13s are $450! I only have one pair left [size nine in men's]. OK< go to the website and get them now.

P: I don't feel guilty because I am giving them access to products they don't have in India.

Both returned to their StockX sales to their customers in India, occasionally high-fiving each other when they secured a big deal. They were like the Tweedles in Alice in Wonderland, finishing each other's sentences and oblivious to the outside world.

****

Ideas can partially explain my reluctant gift exchange with these two passengers in the Lewis Carroll poem, the Walrus and Carpenter. I watched them in the rear-view mirror and immediately slipped into Lewis Carroll's world. Although it's a longer nonsense poem than, say, 'Jabberwocky,' 'The Walrus and the Carpenter' is easy to summarize. The two title characters are walking along a beach. They find a bed of oysters and proceed to eat the entire lot. We are clearly in a nonsense world, a world of fantasy: the sun and the moon are both out on this night.

The oysters (their customers) can walk and even wear shoes, even though they don't have feet. No, they don't have feet, but they have 'heads' described as being in their beds – with 'bed' here going beyond the meaning of 'seabed' instead of conjuring up the absurdly comical idea of the oysters tucked up in bed asleep.

Which of the two Tweedles is the male and female is unclear. One is like the sun, a bold interloper, refusing to set when night comes on and instead boldly and presumptuously encroaching on the moon's bed of oysters.

I tried to use a humorous analogy to endure their noisy antics, and finally, they relented. It took some imagination and creative sensemaking. I told of Lewis Carroll's writings:

Did I mention Tweedledee and Tweedledum (from Alice in Wonderland)? These two young Indian women got into my car and were dressed in amusing ways as if they were going to a private fashion show event with colorful dresses, scarves, and vails. They had lots of makeup on, they wore unusual shoes, and expensive accessories donned to attract (male?) attention and disguise their young age? For what purpose? Grammar school dress like the Tweedles? No! Something even more hilarious, SHOPPING!

I am not sure why I thought of Tweedle-dee and Tweedledum when they got into my car. They were talking so fast and finishing each other's sentences. They were a very mysterious pair in that they were both slightly overweight, appearing round and brandishing their phones like royal scepters. They came from a wealthier [and pompous] place.

My young passengers were like the Walrus and Carpenter; they tricked friends back home into spending exorbitant sums on fashionable apparel. The symbolic seashore these young women walk along is their expensive college campus environs and the upscale apartments they inhabit. They exploit others to serve their worldly needs.

The Walrus and the Carpenter, a narrative poem famous for the themes of death and betrayal, was also mentioned. Published in 1865, the English poem follows two curious characters [Walrus and a Carpenter] who trick innocent young oysters and eat them while walking along the seashore. The poem also deals with the idea of cunning and exploitation in human nature.

They were UM students (seniors) at the University of Michigan. The first thing that came to mind about their behavior and manner was this strange sense of entitlement they commanded like they were the royal princesses visiting America. They needed everyone in their presence (including me) to acknowledge their presumed higher status.

The story of 'The Walrus and the Carpenter', in one sense, is a story of exploitation and entitlement: the sun sits upon the moon's territory or time, the Walrus and the Carpenter upon the oysters, which they presume to eat – because they can.

We might talk of many things, but what remains are the funny images and the delightful play of language – nonsense or otherwise. That is what this trip with the Tweedles descended into silliness and harmless play. However, the two eventually explained what they did to make money for college. As I get older, noise suppression and avoidance of errant noise become more important to me.

I wish to convey that these two young women, in their appearance and revealing how they financed their extravagant college lives, personified something that elevated me. The Tweedles and Lewis Carroll's satirical work lifted my impression of my Lyft driver status. This new understanding of my driver role helped me to self-identify as an author creating my world of fantasy satire and reworking my experiences through the magical interpretation of a great work of literature. It was the stuff of dreams for me as an author, storyteller, and another surprising manifestation of my thirty-day odyssey.

Story Twenty-Nine

The Silent Rider

October 26, 2021

"I have learned silence from the talkative, toleration from the intolerant, and kindness from the unkind; yet, strange, I am ungrateful to those teachers."

-Khalil Gibran, from The Prophet

Of the 325 Lyft rides I have delivered over the 30 days of collecting these stories, this one seemed to annoy me right until the end. I am not sure why it bothered me so much in the beginning. Maybe it was just my imagination. I was tired when I picked up the young man from Planet Fitness. I waited five minutes in the parking lot. The Lyft app prompted me to push the No Show - cancel the ride button. We know how time gets compressed, then your expectations about waiting for change. I find myself getting agitated if the wait extends an extra minute. Was I peeved because I was driving instead of working out at the health club? My back and neck were so sore? I did not feel like waiting for anyone!

I started imagining that this young man who requested a ride had just stepped out of the locker room shower and was still towing himself off when he requested the Lyft ride. He had this expensive [designer] workout suit with his phone in one hand and the towel in the other. Tiredness warps my thinking. He opened the back door, lumbered into my car like he was playing rugby, and did not even say hello as he continued to rub the towel over his head. Then he wrapped the towel around his neck while staring at his phone, not a peep when I asked:

M: Where to?

M: No Answer. He turned and stared at me.

I looked at the GPS routing on the Lyft Home page, which said, "Campus Towers," and since I knew where to go, I just dismissed the awkward beginning. I assumed he was a student.

I tried several times to strike up a conversation with no effect. He was looking down at his phone. I thought to myself, that was what was so different today. The young people stare into their phones and ignore the people in front of them.

I felt a little annoyed. I wasn't used to getting rejected with silence. I imagined he looked up and saw I was a bit peeved but said nothing. When we pulled up to the Campus Towers Building, I was fuming a bit and anxious to have him get out so I could resume my day. Then, he got out of the car. I was about to speed off when he turned and signed "Thank You" and turned away, and I saw he had hearing aids in both of his ears.

How could I have been so ignorant? He was deaf! And then I felt like an idiot. I had assumed he was giving me the silent treatment [which he was] but not for the reasons I thought.

I even rejected the following few ride requests. I needed to calm down. Disappointed in myself, I went offline for a few minutes. I was tired of driving. Lyft driving fatigue was more profound than I had realized. Pain in my back and neck was occurring with more frequency.

I didn't want to sit there and beat myself up for making a dumb mistake. Still, beyond feeling angry for what I imagined happening, I also thought about the passenger having to deal with a frustrated driver trying to communicate with him. I tried to imagine being deaf and having to read people's lips, avoiding getting run over by cars, trucks, and bikes you couldn't hear coming.

I imagined being deaf and Lyft driving. It was challenging to guess how much more vigilant I would need to be with my eyes. How much would I focus my sight on everything around me to keep my passengers safer? Are there any deaf Lyft drivers out there? I wondered. Is it even legal for deaf people to Lyft drive? I imagine it is.

I don't know why I became sensitive about how passengers interacted once they got into my car. Perhaps there is something about strangers entering your territory, invading your space. It makes you feel a bit nervous.

Silent riders made me nervous because most people entering my car would say hello and call me by my name. If they didn't execute that routine, my antennae would go up. I began sizing them up another way.

I wondered how other Lyft drivers feel about silent riders. I had no way of knowing. During the next few weeks, I didn't drive with another silent rider until the thirtieth day. It happened on the last day of my passenger story data collection, the second to the last ride of that day.

When I picked up a middle-aged woman at the UM Hospital on Day thirty, she was on the phone. She said nothing, and I could hear a voice speaking to her as she listened. She was listening, and tears were running down her face. She never looked at me once. I felt like I didn't exist. I was embarrassed to be witnessing her distress and eavesdropping on her conversation. I wanted to disappear. Why? We are sensitive to others, and their emotions are contagious.

I said hello as she got in the car, noticing she was on the phone. The ride was about six minutes. She was on the phone the entire time. I drove her in silence. I do not enjoy these rides at all.

I pulled up to the destination, and she got out, still on the phone, sobbing while she listened. I felt helpless as she exited the car. She walked off in obvious distress. I had no idea what was causing her such anguish or what was said. I was not feeling annoyed. I was invisible.

****

During the first few weeks of Lyft driving, I averaged at least one distressing ride a day. These rides were the signal flares of my physical and psychological condition. These rides were much more taxing and emotionally draining. I can now tell you why. A typical Lyft driving day rolled out like this:

I might start driving at 9 or 10 am. I would have a few local rides, relatively short and low, earning from $3 -$5. I would average around $4.00 in earnings for the first few rides. Usually, two or three until my daily total reached $20-$25. It was slow going and challenging because I felt little earning progress. I was not looking forward to a long day of local driving. What kept me going was not earnings but acquiring some good stories. Sometimes, I didn't get the opportunity to reveal my intent or my identity when serving my Lyft customers. Some passengers entered my car and completely dismissed me. Perhaps they didn't want to interact with "drivers" out of habit or by some twisted assumption that we were strangers and potential exploiters.

Getting into a car with a stranger can certainly be uncomfortable at the very least, especially when an awkward silence is broken only by a finger tapping on one's phone or the only sound occurring during the entire trip is noise coming from the passenger's earphones. For most of this Lyft Driving odyssey, I have successfully engaged my passengers in conversation, knowing it to be my only way of enhancing our ride experience. I figured that if I could get them to share something with me, then we would both enjoy a benefit. I always assumed that people wanted to engage. I was wrong in a few cases. Silent rides are awful. I don't enjoy them, and I never will.

It seemed like a good thing, but only about 5% of my passengers initiated the conversation with me as a Lyft driver. I could tell when passengers were uncomfortable speaking to me. Some would appear annoyed or guarded, while others seemed threatened and were evasive with their eyes. Others quietly stared at their phones.

It was easy for me to remain silent and complete this kind of Lyft ride. I endured the silence sometimes out of courtesy. Some silent riders exited my car and said nothing. No thank you, no goodbye. A small number just got out and slammed the door for no apparent reason. Silent rides bothered me until the next passenger came along, and we began a pleasant conversation.

This Lyft passenger ride disturbed me. Yet over time, I started to understand my poor reaction. Perhaps I need to adapt and learn to accept that not every passenger was friendly and would engage in a conversation. Yet, the very purpose of this work for me was getting good stories.

There is a story in silence. Sure, I wanted my passengers to enjoy their ride with me. Yet, the main reason I started Lyft driving was to experience social activity again after the miserable isolation during the pandemic. My daughter rightly said, Dad, you like to talk to strangers. You get pleasure from conversations about anything. That is your natural gift. During this ride, I discovered how important interacting with my riders was…to me. And I learned something about the gift of silence.

Story Thirty

Up in Michigan

October 27, 2022

"I think we all have our personalities, unique and distinctive at the same time. I believe that our individual and distinct personality blends with the wind, the footsteps in the street, the noises around the corner, and the silence of memory, which is the great producer of ghosts."

-Octavio Paz

Part 1. I picked up Jonathan at the Greyhound Bus Depot in Ann Arbor.

M: Hi Jonathan, just getting back to A2?

P: Yeah, Call me Jon. It was a long bus ride from the UP. I went up to see my mother. She had Covid-19 a few weeks ago. It was hard on her, but she made it through. I went to college at Northern Michigan University in Marquette [NMU].

M: What a coincidence. I went there too. What did you study?

P: Accounting and business, but eventually, I got a master's in education. I sort of fell into it. Now, I hope to land a job as an assistant school principal. How long have you been Lyft driving?

M: One month. I have been busy collecting Lyft passenger stories for a book I am writing. I am a retired business professor [UM]. I have 48 stories so far, and this is the last day to sign up!

P: Wow, that is a large number of stories. I should tell you my crazy story.

M: Well, we have about twenty-five minutes to Farmington, so have a go.

P: OK. After graduating from NMU a few years ago in December, I had no idea what to do next. It was winter, and all I wanted to do was ski and sleep. I had rented this small log cottage right on the Lake. Do you know where Shot Point Road is?

M: Yes, exactly. Just before Sand River and Deerton. I used to take people on hikes I called, Chasing Hemingway's Ghost, where we would trace the Big Two-hearted River right where it spills into Lake Superior. But that is another story. Go on.

P: My undergraduate degree was in accounting, and even though I was pretty good at accounting, I hated doing it. So, I thought I might look at the graduate programs at NMU.

M: The NMU Registrar told me that there was only one graduate course available to enroll in if you had not been accepted in a graduate program. The course was ED 500, taught by Dr. L. Thayer [T], titled Educational Research. I had no clue what that entailed, but I signed up anyway.

M: I sat in that class for twelve weeks and did not understand what Dr. Thayer was teaching. It was like he spoke a different language. The entire point of this course was to develop a research proposal, so everything he lectured about was called research methods. I was vexed.

M: The single assignment due in week thirteen was this proposal to research an education topic. I had no issue; therefore, I had no proposal. The week the submission was due, I panicked. Then, I was reading the campus newspaper and a topic suddenly appeared. Long story short, I submitted a poorly conceived, error-ridden, twelve-page document. I didn't know what I was doing, but I managed to submit something. When Dr. Thayer returned the papers the following week, I received a note instructing me to visit his office immediately after class. I entered Dr. Thayer's office, and he attended to the papers on his desk without looking up. I sat down directly across from him. After a few unsettling minutes, he picked up my paper and tossed it in my lap. Then he said, Mr. Peters, You need to think about doing something else."

P: Something besides researching NMU's institutional role? And Dr. Thayer said, No, something besides graduate study. I felt like I had been gut-punched. My paper must have been awful.

M: Dr. Thayer returned to his paperwork. I realized he was dismissing me. I sat there and waited for more of an explanation. A painful ten minutes went by without a word. Dr. Thayer looked over his glasses and said, OK, Mr. Peters, I will give you precisely seven days, one week to write an acceptable draft proposal, or do not bother returning to the last class of the course. He looked at his watch and marked the time. Seven days.

M: I stepped into the hallway with a lump in my throat. I wasn't sure what to do next. I stepped out in the Marquette cold, and the winter wind off the Lake went right through me. I shivered and realized I should get out of the cold, so I went into the library. I spied one of my recreation buddies [Kevin] who worked there. Hey, Peters. What are you doing these days?

I just got my ass kicked by Dr. Thayer, I said. I signed up for ED 500 and didn't know what I was doing. We are supposed to write a research proposal. I never did anything like that before. Any ideas? He looked at me and lit up. Wait, I will be right back. Kevin reemerged in about ten minutes with this stack of books. He said, here, start with this. How to Write a Research Proposal. Catchy title.

M: Kevin loaded about fifteen books in my arms, and I returned to my lakefront cabin. It was mid-April, yet there was little sign of spring thaw. I walked along the near-frozen shoreline; the enormous blocks of water ice swayed back and forth. The water beyond churned a chalky grey with white-top waves curling over the harbor break wall in the distance. I was mesmerized by it all. I was looking out at the expanse, hoping to draw inspiration.

M: For the next six days, I did nothing but scour the books Kevin gave me. I followed page by page and crafted the proposal, sometimes working sixteen hours daily. I would show Dr. Thayer that I wasn't a poser. After about five days, a draft began to emerge. I gained some confidence by attempting the literature review. The method section I nearly copied [I cited everything I used].

M: The Friday evening it was due, instead of attending class, I had the department secretary time-stamped my paper, then she placed it in Dr. Thayer's department mailbox.

M: The course ended the last week of April. I received a B in the course with no other acknowledgment from Dr. Thayer. I didn't hear anything from NMU for weeks. After I turned in a 36-page proposal to study the newly designated dual-role of Northern Michigan University as a four-year university and regional community college, I thought, well, that was too work for a lousy B grade [Perhaps I should have been grateful since I had acquired the proposal issue from casually reading the NMU student newspaper].

M: One day in mid-May, my mother called me. She was the only person that had my phone number. Both of my parents got on the line. My mother said NMU called here and wanted to speak with you. It was the Vice President of Academic Affairs calling. He asked if I could pass along an invitation for me to attend a nine o'clock meeting the next day at his office? My father chimed in by saying, "Do you still have that sports coat I bought? Better get dressed up for the execution! Ha ha, that's funny, dad.

M: The next day, I walked into the VP's office, and he joyfully said, Come, let's visit with the President. I became nervous. He rose as we entered the President's office, holding up a document.

M: Hello Mr. Peters, I understand you wrote this proposal for Dr. Thayer's course? Yes, that is correct. Can I ask you what this is about?

M: Indeed, we have done a little investigating and want to offer you an opportunity. How would you like to execute your proposal and enroll in a master's program aligned with this very issue, and of course, we will find a way to pay for it?

M: Wow, you can do that? Then I heard chuckling. I was suddenly aware several other people were in the room sitting in wing chairs behind me. Dr. Thayer was nowhere to be seen.

M: We want you to be the student representative on a President's Task Force exploring and clarifying this important issue. Are you interested? I am. Can I talk this over with my family and get back to you tomorrow with my answer? Certainly.

M: I admit this offer came out of the blue. I was dumbfounded. My parents were filled with joy when I told them what had happened. I guessed that Dr. Thayer passed my proposal along, thinking it was good enough to present to the administration.

Part 2.

M: Of course, I accepted the President's offer. What dumb luck it was to be offered such a fantastic role. I wasn't looking forward to moving onto campus by mid-June and giving up my lake-front cabin rental. I loved living there.

The following two years went by like a Midwestern thunderstorm. I became wholly absorbed in the study of educational administration. I sat on academic committees and participated in endless faculty meetings learning the political dynamics surrounding this issue. I was fully engaged. When it came time to write my master's thesis, I never felt so prepared. I planned to clarify this issue single-handedly and perhaps present my research to the State of Michigan Senate. I didn't do much of anything but work.

Then one day, I ran into my friend Kevin. He had heard that I was working on the President's Task Force and wanted to know how I was doing? He asked me a strange question that jolted me. "Are you having any fun besides working for the Top Brass, as he called them? I thought about it and sheepishly said no.

M: Hey, you know what you need to do? Go over to the new deli store called Esperanto and get yourself some exotic treats from far places like Paraguay and Moldova. They have all kinds of delicacies perfect for lonely, suffering graduate students! OK, I will.

M: The next day, I walked down to this little Esperanto store, as Kevin suggested. I perused the shelves full of jars of spiced fruits, bottled oils, and different kinds of vinegar, olives, and peppers from all over the world. I loved these foods but always thought they were too extravagant and expensive; then I heard Kevin's voice in my head egging me on.

I stood along the wall looking toward the kitchen area when I saw a young woman chopping vegetables and preparing food. She was beautiful, and I could not keep my eyes off her. I realized I was staring at her and retreated into the aisles. I grabbed a wrapped spinach croissant from the counter and made my way out.

When I stepped out the door into the street, I once again felt I had been gut-punched. I stood there on the sidewalk, wondering why I didn't have a girlfriend? Why didn't I have a girlfriend like the woman in the store?

A few days later, I returned to the store like a lost puppy. I immediately noticed the absence of the young woman working in the kitchen. How can I help you today, asked the woman working behind the deli counter? Is the young woman I saw working here the other day? No, she will be back on Friday, though, if you come back then. She winked at me!

I was hilarious the next time I went to the store that Friday afternoon. AS soon as the older woman saw me enter the store, she went to the kitchen and instructed the younger woman, named Maria, to go to the cash register. I grabbed any old jar of something and headed to pay. Maria stared at me, saying she didn't know how to work the register.

I was puzzled, wondering why on Earth would they have her work the register if she didn't know how to do it. So, I said to her. It is easy. You punch up the price, accept the money from the customer, and give them their change based on how much money they give you minus the item's price. Simple, yes? She smiled at me, and my heart fluttered. When she looked at me, I became slightly disoriented and dumber than usual. Then Maria said something surprising. She asked me if I would like to go running. I didn't tell her I was not much of a runner, so I said sure. She told me to give her my number, and she would call me.

I left suddenly feeling intoxicated. My swooning was tempered by thinking she was probably being polite and would not call. However, the next day she did. I am not looking for a boyfriend was the first thing she said to me. I need a running partner if you are interested. I mentioned that I was going rock climbing the following day if she wanted to come along. We'll meet at six am. Is that too early? Sure, I would love to go rock climbing.

We had a great time climbing the back side of Marquette Mountain Ski Hill. I showed her how to set up a top-rope climbing system, and she showed me how to climb a cliff like a spider. She was talented and had climbed before. She told me she still wanted a running partner, so we ran in the rain the next day. It was very romantic, and we both knew something was happening we didn't expect.

Just before dropping Maria at home because it started pouring, she asked me if I wanted to help her make lasagna for a senior home in Marquette. We have been together ever since that day.

I presented my master's thesis project to the NMU community the following spring. Maria was there with several dignitaries from the Michigan government and other educational institutions around the state. NMU's president held court, and they all thought my work was outstanding. Even Dr. Thayer attended, demonstrating his approval of my work and acceptance of me as a colleague.

Dr. Thayer told me he had a confession to make. Do you know why I treated you so poorly when we first met in ED 500? I said no, sir. I thought you didn't like me. Nonsense, he said. I rejected you because I thought you were a local journalist sent to spy on me and collect information about the NMU dual-role subject. You see, merely two weeks before you submitted your inferior draft proposal, the NMU president appointed me the head of his

Task Force charged with redefining NMU's role. I had no idea. Of course, you didn't. You see, I earned a Master of Arts degree AND met my future wife by fortunate accident. That is what amazes me. How could a big lug like me be so lucky? Good thing this all happened a few years before the pandemic hit. I would probably still live alone in that cabin up in Michigan chasing after Hemingway's ghost.

EPILOGUE

When I started Lyft driving, I felt reluctant about it. I had no plan or approach. The idea of writing a book had not emerged. I remember my wife telling me that first day to be open to the experience. That was one little push, then hearing story one and feeling compelled to write it down was another, and then my phone call with Esther Wojcicki sealed it. I am a writer that merely happened to Lyft drive.

One of my early reviewers noted: All thirty stories are so different. What is the message you want readers to hear? What does this collection of passenger stories mean? I can only say that I tried to faithfully represent the conversations I had with Lyft passengers over a designated monthlong period. It is a detailed account of various discussions, and included are a few of my own stories connected to particular themes that emerged during that magical month.

I am not arguing that I know how to be the best Lyft driver, yet I am sharing how I approached this work as I jobcrafted the ridesharing driver role. It was astonishing how the experience of Lyft driving changed my perspectives about the pandemic, work in general, management and organization, and how to better connect with those I interact with daily.

I am proud of myself for creating something of use [a book] from virtually nothing. I enjoyed the writing experience because I found consistent pleasure in listening to passengers. Most were so generous. I felt grateful and fortunate. I will be even more thankful if readers find my stories insightful and my words helpful.

What was helpful for me as I slowly became the Mad Hatter from driving fatigue was connecting my own Lyft driving odyssey to the fantasy and humor of Lewis Carroll. I included passages from his work because they helped me cope with long days of driving, and listening to passenger stories that were uneventful or just plain dull. The great stories were a rarity, yet I enjoyed interacting with all my passengers immensely.

One academic note, if you are up for it. The underlying thread of this book is an example of how I learned to understand complex phenomena [and organizing dynamics] from professors like Michael Cohen and Marvin Peterson at the University of Michigan in the mid-1990s.

I developed an organizational study framework with their help. It consisted of four lenses: variation, interaction, selection, and retention. I actually employed this framework in writing this book as it helped me identify the pattern that connects (Bateson). I captured variation by collecting numerous passenger stories, then I discussed and illuminated certain interactions I had with the passengers, and discovered a few interesting patterns [for selection]. Then I tried to explain what stuck [retention] as patterns emerged during story collecting. It was observing culture through organizing threads and communication patterns.

Of course you must forgive me as I tell you this at the end. Now, you have to read the stories again with what I just told you in mind. Then you can determine for yourself how well...I succeeded!